The Buddha's Path

Nina van Gorkom

1994

Triple Gem Press

Published in April 1994 by:
Triple Gem Press
43 Drakefield Road
Tooting Bec
London
SW17 8RT

© Nina van Gorkom
All rights reserved

British Library Cataloguing in Publication Data

A CIP record for this book is available from the British Library.

ISBN 1 897633 12 2

Printed and bound in Great Britain by
Biddles Limited, Guildford and King's Lynn.

Designed and typeset by Triple Gem Press
in 10/13 bookman.

Front cover: Town centre, Guildford, England.
© photograph by Alan Weller

Contents

- 5 • *Preface*
- 9 • Chapter 1
  Introduction
- 23 • Chapter 2
  The truth of suffering
- 35 • Chapter 3
  The truth of non-self
- 51 • Chapter 4
  The mind
- 67 • Chapter 5
  Deeds and their results
- 83 • Chapter 6
  Good deeds and a wholesome life
- 103 • Chapter 7
  Mental development and meditation
- 123 • Chapter 8
  The eightfold Path
- 143 • *Selected texts*
- 151 • *Glossary*
- 153 • *Index*

Preface

What is Buddhism? It is different from what most people believe: an Oriental religion full of rituals and ceremonies, which teaches meditation leading to mystical experiences. Buddhism is most practical and matter of fact. The Buddha taught all that is real, all mental phenomena and physical phenomena of our life. By the study of his teachings one learns to investigate one's different mental states which change very rapidly. One comes to know one's faults and vices, even the more subtle ones which are not easily noticeable. One learns what is good and wholesome and how to develop wholesome deeds, speech and thoughts. The Buddha taught on life and death, on the conditions for all phenomena which arise and which are impermanent. He pointed out the suffering and dissatisfaction inherent in the phenomena of life. He explained the true nature of man: a composition of elements which arise and then fall away immediately and which are devoid of an abiding substance, of a "self". The Buddha taught the eightfold Path which, if it is developed in the right way, leads to direct understanding of the true nature of all the phenomena of life. It is by direct understanding that defilements can eventually be eradicated.

In this book I try to explain the message, the basic contents and some details of the Buddha's teachings. What is the use of learning details? The Buddha's teachings are subtle and deep and therefore it is necessary to go into details. If one does not know that there are many different aspects to each reality the Buddha taught one will read the scriptures with wrong understanding. There will be an over-simplification in the interpretation of the texts. Patience is needed to grasp the complexity of the teachings in order to avoid a superficial understanding of them. Wrong interpretation of the texts leads to wrong practice of the Buddha's Path, and as a consequence there will not be right understanding of the phenomena within ourselves and around ourselves. The development of the eightfold Path is the development of direct understanding of the true nature of realities. When the way of its development is correctly understood, the truth of what the Buddha taught can be verified through one's own experience. Although theoretical understanding is the foundation for the development of the Path, it is not sufficient to grasp the deep meaning of the teachings. One should know that it takes time and patience to understand what this Path is and how one can begin to develop it.

What is the origin of the Buddhist texts of the Theravāda tradition as they have come to us today? These texts date from the Buddha's time, about 2500 years ago. Shortly after the Buddha's passing away a Council was held in Rājagaha, were the teachings were examined and scrutinized as to their orthodoxy. Under the leadership of the Buddha's eminent disciple Mahā Kassapa five hundred monks who had reached the state of perfection recited all the texts of the Vinaya, the Book of Discipline for the monks, the Suttanta, Discourses, and the Abhidhamma, the higher teaching on ultimate realities. A second Council was held one century later at Vesāli. This was necessary because of wrong interpretations to the monks's rules by heretical monks. A third Council was held in 268 B.C. in Pātalīputta. On this occasion the canon of the Theravāda tradition in the Pāli language as it exists today was finally redacted. During all this time the teachings were handed down by oral tradition. About 89 B.C. they were committed to writing in Sri Lanka.

In this book I have used a few Pāli terms which can be of use to those who intend to deepen their knowledge of Buddhism. The English equivalents of the Pāli terms are often unsatisfactory since they stem from Western philosophy and therefore give an association of meaning which is different from the meaning intended by the Buddhist teachings.

I want to acknowledge my deep gratitude to Ms. Sujin Boriharnwanaket in Thailand, who gave me great assistance in the understanding of the Buddhist teachings and in particular in their application. I also wish to express my gratitude to the "Dhamma Study and Propagation Foundation", to the publisher Alan Weller and to my husband. Without their help the writing and the printing of this book would not have been possible.

Finally I want to give information on the sources of my quotations from the texts in the English language. I quoted mainly from the *Dialogues of the Buddha*, the *Middle Length Sayings*, the *Kindred Sayings* and the *Gradual Sayings*. I also quoted from the *Path of Purification* which is an Encyclopedia on Buddhism written by the commentator Buddhaghosa in the fifth century A.D. This is only a selection of the texts I used. They are available at the Pāli Text Society, 73 Lime Walk, Headington, Oxford OX3 7AD, England.

With this book I intend to give an introduction to the Buddhist teachings. I hope that I can encourage readers to explore the scriptures themselves in order to deepen their own understanding.

Nina van Gorkom.

Chapter I

Introduction

Why are we in this life? Why do we have to suffer? Men of all times conceived philosophical systems which could explain the reason for their existence and give a solution to the problem of suffering. Religions also try to give an answer to the problem of suffering in teaching that people should have faith in God and live according to His commandments; consequently one can, after death, enjoy eternal bliss in heaven. The Buddha gave his own, unique answer to the problem of suffering. He taught that the cause of suffering is within man, namely his own faults and defilements, and not in the external situation. He explained that only profound knowledge of his own mind and of all phenomena of his life can lead to the end of suffering. We read in the Buddhist scriptures (Kindred Sayings I, Chapter II, Part 3, §3, The World) that King Pasenadi had a conversation with the Buddha at Sāvatthī about the cause of suffering. We read:

"...How many kinds of things, lord, that happen in the world, make for
trouble, for suffering, for distress?"
"Three things, sire, happen of that nature. What are the three?
Greed, hate, and delusion—these three make for trouble, for
suffering, for distress..."

The outward circumstances cannot be changed, but the inward attitude towards the vicissitudes of life can be changed. Wisdom can be developed and this can eventually eradicate completely greed, hate and delusion. This wisdom is not developed by speculation about the truth of life, it is developed through the direct experience of the phenomena of life as they really are, including one's own mental states. That is the Path the Buddha taught, but it takes time to understand how it is to be developed.

The Buddha was not a God, not a saviour, who wanted people to follow him without questioning the truth of his teaching. He showed the Path to the understanding of the truth, but people had to investigate the truth and develop the Path themselves. We read in the scriptures (Dialogues of the Buddha, II, 16, the Book of the Great Decease) that the Buddha said to his disciple Ānanda:

> *Therefore, Ānanda, be an island to yourselves, a refuge to yourselves, seeking no external refuge; with the Teaching as your island, the Teaching as your refuge, seeking no other refuge...*

The Buddha explained that in developing the Path one is one's own refuge.

The Buddha had found the Path to understanding of the truth all by himself, without help from a teacher. However, he was not the only Buddha. Aeons and aeons ago there were other Buddhas who also found the Path all by themselves and who taught the development of the Path to others. The Buddha whose teaching we know in this time was called the Buddha Gotama. His personal name was Siddhattha and his family name Gotama. He lived in the sixth century B.C. in Northern India. He was born in Lumbini (now in Nepal) as the son of Suddhodana, King of the Sākyas. His mother was Queen Māyā. He married Princess Yasodhārā and he lived in great luxury. However, when he drove out to the park with his charioteer he was confronted with suffering. We read in the *Dialogues of the Buddha* (II, 14, The Sublime Story) that also former

Buddhas had such experiences. In this sutta we read that the Buddha related the story of a former Buddha, the Buddha Vipassi, and explained that all Bodhisattas, beings destined to become Enlightened Ones, Buddhas, have the same experiences. We read that the Bodhisatta, after he saw in the park someone who was aged, asked the charioteer the meaning of what he saw. The charioteer explained to him that the person he saw was aged and that all beings are subject to old age. On a following occasion there was an encounter with a sick person and the charioteer explained that all beings are subject to illness. At another occasion the Bodhisatta saw a corpse. The charioteer explained that that was the corpse of someone who had ended his days. We read:

> ...And Vipassi saw the corpse of him who had ended his days and asked—"What, good charioteer, is ending one's days?"
> "It means, my lord, that neither mother, nor father, nor other kinsfolk will see him any more, nor will he ever see them."
> "But am I too then subject to death, have I not got beyond the reach of death? Will neither the King, nor the Queen, nor any other of my relatives see me any more, or I ever again see them?"
> "You, my lord, and we too, we all are subject to death, we have not passed beyond the reach of death. Neither the King, nor the Queen, nor any other of your relatives would see you any more, nor would you ever again see them."
> "Why then, good charioteer, enough of the park for today! Drive me back from here to my rooms."
> "Yes, my lord," replied the charioteer, and drove him back.
> And he, monks, going to his rooms, sat brooding sorrowful and depressed, thinking—"Shame then verily be upon this thing called birth, since to one born the decay of life, disease and death show themselves like that."

After the Bodhisatta had been confronted with an old man, a sick man and a corpse, his fourth encounter was with a monk. The Bodhisatta asked the meaning of being a monk and the charioteer answered that it was being thorough in the religious life, in the peaceful life, in good actions, in meritorious conduct, in harmlessness, and in kindness to all creatures. The Bodhisatta decided to leave his worldly life and to become a monk.

The Buddha Gotama, when he was still a Bodhisatta, had the same encounters as the Bodhisatta Vipassi. He also became a monk after his fourth encounter in order to seek the solution to the problem of suffering. He first practised severe austerity, but he saw that that was not the way to find the truth. He decided to discontinue such severe practices and to stop fasting. On the day he was to attain enlightenment he took rice gruel which was offered to him by the girl Sujātā. Seated under the Bodhi-tree he attained enlightenment. He realized the four noble Truths: the truth of suffering, of the cause of suffering, of the ceasing of suffering and of the Path leading to the ceasing of suffering. He had attained enlightenment at the age of thirty-five years and he taught the Path to others for forty-five years. At the age of eighty he passed away at Kusinārā.

His teachings have been preserved in the Buddhist scriptures of the Vinaya (Book of Discipline for the monks), the Suttas (the Discourses), and the Abhidhamma (the "Higher Teachings"). These scriptures which have been written in the Pāli language are of the Theravāda tradition. The term "Theravāda" (Hīnayāna or "Small vehicle" is no longer used) could be translated as "the School of the Elders". There is also the Mahāyāna tradition which developed later on. The two traditions are in agreement with several points of the Buddha's teachings, but they are different as regards the practice, the development of the Buddha's Path leading to the realization of the truth. The Theravāda tradition is followed in Thailand, Sri Lanka, Laos, Cambodia and Bangladesh. The Mahāyāna tradition is followed in China, Japan, Tibet and Mongolia.

The Buddha, at his enlightenment, understood that the cause of suffering is craving. He saw that when there is the cessation of craving there will be an end to suffering. What the Buddha teaches is contrary to what people generally are seeking in life. Every being has craving for the experience of pleasant things and therefore wishes to continue to obtain such objects. The Buddha was, after his enlightenment, for a moment not inclined to teach the truth he had realized under the Bodhi-tree. He knew that the "Dhamma", his teaching of the truth, would be difficult to understand by those who delighted in sense pleasures. We read in the *Middle Length Sayings* (I, number 26, The Ariyan Quest), that the Buddha related to the monks his quest for the truth when he was still a Bodhisatta, he spoke about his enlightenment and his disinclination to teaching. We read that the Buddha said:

> *This that through many toils I've won—*
> *Enough! Why should I make it known?*
> *By folk with lust and hate consumed*
> *This Dhamma is not understood.*
> *Leading on against the stream*
> *Deep, subtle, fine, and hard to see,*
> *Unseen it will be by passion's slaves*
> *Cloaked in the murk of ignorance.*

We then read that the Brahmā Sahampati, a heavenly being, implored the Buddha to teach the truth. The Buddha surveyed the world with the eye of an Awakened

One, and he saw beings with different dispositions, some of whom were not capable to accept his teaching, and some who were capable to be taught. We read that the Buddha used a simile of different kinds of lotuses in a pond:

> ...Even as in a pond of blue lotuses or in a pond of red lotuses or in a pond of white lotuses, a few red and blue and white lotuses are born in the water, grow in the water, do not rise above the water but thrive while altogether immersed; a few blue or red or white lotuses are born in the water, grow in the water and reach the surface of the water; a few blue or red or white lotuses are born in the water, grow in the water, and stand rising out of the water, undefiled by the water; even so did I, monks, surveying the world with the eye of an Awakened One, see beings with little dust in their eyes, with much dust in their eyes, with acute faculties, with dull faculties, of good dispositions, of bad dispositions, docile, indocile, few seeing fear in sins and the world beyond.

Out of compassion the Buddha decided to teach Dhamma. His teaching is "against the stream", it is deep and it can only be understood by studying it thoroughly and by carefully considering it. Generally, people expect something else from the Buddhist teachings. They believe that the Buddha taught a method of meditation to reach tranquillity, or even extraordinary experiences such as a mystical trance. It is understandable that one looks for a way of escape from a life full of tension and troubles. Extraordinary experiences, however, cannot give the real solution to one's problems. It is a wrong conception of Buddhism to think that the goal of the Buddha's Path are mystical experiences to be reached by concentration. The Buddha's Path has nothing to do with unworldly mysticism, it is very concrete and matter of fact. Understanding should be developed of all that is real, also of our faults and vices as they naturally appear during our daily activities. We have to know ourselves when we laugh, when we cry, when we are greedy or angry, we have to know all our different moods. All troubles in life are caused by our defilements. It is through the development of understanding that defilements can be completely eradicated. Comprehending, knowing and seeing are stressed time and again in the Buddhist teachings.

It is felt by some people that, in order to develop understanding of one's mind, one should retire from daily life and sit still in quiet surroundings. It may seem that, when one is in isolation, there is no anger or aversion and that it is easier to analyse one's mental states. However, at such moments there is bound to be clinging to quietness and when there is clinging there is no development of understanding. We read in the scriptures about people who could develop calm in concentrating on a meditation subject. They were very skilled, they knew the right method to attain calm, which is a wholesome mental state. However, through the development of calm defilements are not eradicated, they are merely temporarily suppressed. The Buddha taught the way to develop the understanding leading to the complete and final eradication of all that is impure, of all defilements. In order to reach the goal there is no other way but developing understanding naturally in one's daily life.

It cannot be expected that there will be the eradication of defilements soon since they are so deeply rooted. The Buddha had, during countless lives when he was still a Bodhisatta, developed understanding of all phenomena of life. Only in his last life, at the moment he attained enlightenment, all defilements were eradicated. How could we expect to reach the final goal within a short time?

The Buddha taught the way to the eradication of all

defilements. Defilements are not eradicated by rituals or by sacraments. The way to eradicate them is an inner way, namely the understanding of all mental and physical phenomena of one's life. The Buddha taught very precisely what defilements are. They are not exactly the same as what is generally meant by "sin". By sin is usually meant an evil deed, evil speech or evil thought which has a high degree of impurity. According to the Buddhist teachings defilements include all degrees, even slight degrees, of what is impure. Even slight degrees of defilements are unhelpful, not beneficial. The term "unwholesomeness", that which is unhelpful, not beneficial, includes all degrees of defilements[1]. If one thinks in terms of sin one will not understand that ignorance of the phenomena of life is unwholesome, that ignorance is harmful since it blinds one to see the truth. Or one will not understand that even a slight degree of attachment is unwholesome, even harmful, because it is accumulated and therefore will arise again and again.

The Buddha, when he was sitting under the Bodhi-tree, realized the four noble Truths: the Truth of suffering, the Truth of the origin of suffering, the Truth of the ceasing of suffering, and the Truth of the Path leading to the ceasing of suffering. As to the Truth of suffering, this is not merely suffering caused by bodily and mental pain. The Truth of suffering pertains to all phenomena of life which are impermanent. They arise and then fall away immediately, and thus they cannot be our refuge. Suffering in this sense is the unsatisfactoriness inherent in all phenomena of life. The Truth of suffering can only be realized when the arising and falling away of physical phenomena and mental phenomena can be directly experienced.

---

[1] "Unwholesome" and "wholesome" are terms which usually stand for the Pāli terms "akusala" and "kusala".

The Truth of the origin of suffering is craving. Craving in this sense is not only strong attachment or greed, it includes many shades and degrees of attachment. There is craving for pleasant colours, sounds, odours, flavours and tangible objects, for all that can be experienced through the senses. There is craving for the continuation of life. It is craving which conditions rebirth in new existences, again and again. Craving pushes beings on in the cycle of life, the continuation of rebirth and death. There is not only this present life, there were also past lives and there will be future lives. I will deal with this subject later on. So long as there are ignorance and clinging there are conditions for being in the cycle of birth and death. Through wisdom, understanding, there can be liberation from it. When there are no more conditions for rebirth, there is the end of old age, sickness and death, the end of all suffering.

The third noble Truth, the cessation of suffering, is nibbāna. The Buddha experienced at his enlightenment nibbāna. It is difficult to understand what nibbāna, is. Nibbāna (more popularly known in its Sanskrit form of nirvāṇa), is not a place such as heaven or a paradise where one enjoys eternal bliss. There are heavenly planes, according to the Buddhist teachings, where one can be reborn as a result of a good deed, but existence in such planes is not forever. After one's lifespan in such a plane is ended there will be rebirth in other planes, and thus there is no end to suffering. Nibbāna is only an object of speculation so long as it has not been realized. It can be realized when there is full understanding of all phenomena of life which arise because of their own conditions and then fall away. The conditioned phenomena of life are, because of their impermanence, unsatisfactory or suffering. Nibbāna is the unconditioned reality, it does not arise and fall away and therefore it is not suffering, it is the end of suffering. Nibbāna is real, it is a reality which can be experienced, but we cannot grasp what an unconditioned reality is when we have not realized the truth of conditioned realities. Nibbāna is not a God, it is not a person or a self. Since negative terms are used to express what nibbāna is, such as the end of rebirth, it may be felt that Buddhism propagates a negative attitude towards life. However, this is not the case. It has to be understood that rebirth is suffering and that nibbāna is the end of suffering. Nibbāna is freedom from all defilements, and since defilements are the cause of all unhappiness nibbāna should be called the highest goal. We read in the *Kindred Sayings* (IV, Kindred Sayings on Sense, Part IV, Chapter 38, §1, Nibbāna) that the wanderer Rose-apple-eater came to see the Buddha's disciple Sāriputta and asked him what nibbāna was. Sāriputta answered:

> The destruction of lust, the destruction of hatred, the destruction of illusion, friend, is called nibbāna.

"Extinction" and "freedom from desire" are meanings of the word nibbāna. Nibbāna means the end of clinging to existence and thus it is deliverance from all future birth, old age, sickness and death, from all suffering which is inherent in the conditioned realities of life. The Buddha experienced at his enlightenment the unconditioned reality which is nibbāna. His passing away was the absolute extinguishment of conditions for the continuation of the life process. This is called his "parinibbāna". When the Buddha was still alive people asked him what would happen to him after his passing away. He explained that this belongs to the questions which cannot be answered, questions which are merely speculative and do not lead to the goal. The Buddha's passing away cannot be called the annihilation of life, nor can there be rebirth for him in another plane. If there would be rebirth he would not have reached the end of all suffering.

The fourth noble Truth, the way leading to the ceasing of suffering, is the development of the eightfold Path as taught by the Buddha. I will deal with the eightfold Path more extensively later on in this book. The eightfold Path is the development of understanding of all physical phenomena and mental phenomena which occur in daily life. Very gradually these phenomena can be realized as impermanent, suffering and "not self". The Buddha taught that there is in the absolute sense no abiding person or self. What is generally understood as a person is merely a temporary combination of mental phenomena and physical phenomena which arise and fall away. The Buddha's teaching of the truth of "non self" is deep and difficult to grasp. This teaching is unique and cannot be found in other philosophical systems or religions. I will deal with the truth of "non self" later on in this book. So long as there is still clinging to the concept of a self defilements cannot be eradicated. There has to be first the eradication of the wrong view of self and then other defilements can be eradicated stage by stage.

There were many monks, nuns and laypeople who developed the Path and realized the goal, each in their own situation. The development of the eightfold Path does not mean that one should try to be detached immediately from all pleasant objects and from existence. All realities, including attachment, should be known and understood. So long as there are conditions for attachment it arises. The development of understanding cannot be forced, it must be done in a natural way. Only thus can understanding, knowing and seeing, very gradually lead to detachment. When one is a layfollower one enjoys all the pleasant things of life, but understanding of realities can be developed. The monk who observes the rules of monkhood leads a different kind of life, but this does not mean that he already is without attachment to pleasant objects. He too should develop understanding naturally, in his own situation, and come to know his own defilements.

The development of the Buddha's Path is very gradual, it is a difficult and long way. It may take many lives before there can be the attainment of enlightenment. Since the development of the Path is so difficult there may be doubt whether it makes sense to start on this Path. It is complicated to understand all phenomena of life, including our own mental states, and it seems impossible to eradicate defilements. It is useless to expect results soon, but it is beneficial to start to investigate what our life really is: phenomena which are impermanent and thus unsatisfactory. When we start on the Buddha's Path we begin to see our many faults and vices, not only the coarse ones but also the more subtle ones which may not have been so obvious. Before studying the Buddhist teachings, selfish motives when performing deeds of generosity were unnoticed. When the deep, underlying, impure motives for one's deeds are realized is that not a gain? A sudden change of character cannot be expected soon as a result of the Buddhist teachings, but what is unwholesome can be realized as unwholesome, and what is wholesome can be realized as wholesome. In that way there will be more truthfulness, more sincerity in our actions, speech and thoughts. The disadvantage and danger of unwholesomeness and the benefit of wholesomeness will be seen more and more clearly.

The Buddha taught about everything which is real and which can be experienced in daily life. He taught about seeing and hearing, about all that can be experienced through the senses. He taught that on account of what is experienced through the senses there is attachment, aversion and ignorance. We are ignorant most of the time of the phenomena occurring in daily life. However, even when we only begin to develop understanding we can verify the truth of what the Buddha taught. Seeing, hearing, attachment, anger, generosity and kindness are real for everybody. There is no need to label what is true for everybody as "Buddhism". When we begin to investigate what the Buddha taught there will gradually be the elimination of ignorance about ourselves and the world around us.

We read in the *Kindred Sayings* (IV, Kindred Sayings on Sense, The Third Fifty, Chapter I, §111, Understanding):

By not comprehending, by not understanding, without detaching himself from, without abandoning the eye, one is incapable of the destruction of suffering. By not comprehending...the ear...nose...tongue...body...mind...one is incapable of the destruction of suffering.

But by comprehending, by understanding, by detaching himself from, by abandoning the eye...nose...tongue...body...mind...one is capable of the destruction of suffering.

In the following sutta we read that, for the destruction of suffering colours, sounds, scents, savours, tangible objects and mind-states have to be understood. This is the way leading to the end of suffering. The Buddha taught about realities for the sake of our welfare and happiness.

Chapter 2

The truth of suffering

Old age, sickness and death are unavoidable. Separation from dear people through death is bound to happen. We read in the *Group of Discourses* (Sutta-Nipāta, III, 8, The Arrow, verses 574-582[2]):

Unindicated and unknown is the length of life of those subject to death. Life is difficult and brief and bound up with suffering. There is no means by which those who are born will not die. Having reached old age, there is death. This is the natural course for a living being. With ripe fruits there is the constant danger that they will fall. In the same way, for those born and subject to death, there is always the fear of dying. Just as the pots made by a potter all end by being broken, so death is the breaking up of life...

The young and old, the foolish and the wise, all are stopped short by the power of death, all finally end in death. Of those overcome by death and passing to another world, a father cannot hold back his son, nor relatives a relation. See! While the relatives are looking on and weeping, one by one each mortal is led away like an ox to the slaughter.

In this manner the world is afflicted by death and decay. But the wise do not grieve, having realized the nature of the world...

The Buddha consoled those who had suffered the loss of dear people by explaining to them the impermanence of all phenomena of life. We read in the commentary to the *Psalms of the Sisters* (Therīgāthā, Canto X) that a woman, named Kisā-gotamī, was completely overwhelmed by grief

---
[2] I am using the translation of J. Ireland, Wheel Publication 82.

because of the loss of her son. She went from door to door with his corpse asking for medicine which could revive him. The Buddha said to her: "Go, enter the town, and bring from any house where yet no man has died a little mustard seed." She did not find any family without bereavement caused by death and she realized that everything is impermanent. She went to the Buddha and he said:

> *To him whose heart on children and on goods*
> *Is centred, clinging to them in his thoughts,*
> *Death comes like a great flood in the night,*
> *Bearing away the village in its sleep.*

Did the Buddha teach anything new? We all know that there has to be separation and death, that everything in life is impermanent. Thinking about impermanence is not of much help when one has suffered a loss. The Buddha taught that there is change of mental states from moment to moment and that also the physical units which constitute the body are breaking up from moment to moment. He taught the development of the wisdom which is the direct experience of the arising and falling away of mental phenomena and physical phenomena. Kisā-gotamī did not merely think about the impermanence of life, she realized through direct experience the momentary breaking up of the mental phenomena and the physical phenomena. This changed her outlook on life and she could recover from her deep sorrow.

Each mental state which arises falls away within split-seconds. At one moment we may speak kindly to someone else but the next moment the kind disposition has disappeared and we may be irritated and angry, we may even shout. It is as if we are a completely different personality at that moment. Actually this is true. Kindness has disappeared and the angry disposition is a different mental state which has arisen. Seeing, hearing or thinking are all different moments of consciousness which arise and then fall away immediately. They each arise because of their own conditioning factors. Seeing, for example is dependant on eye-sense and on its object, which is colour, and since these conditioning factors do not last, also the seeing which is conditioned by them cannot last either. Every reality which is dependant on conditions has to fall away. Since the moment of consciousness which has fallen away is followed by a new one it seems that there is a mind which lasts. In reality our life is an unbroken series of moments of consciousness which arise and fall away. Also bodily phenomena which arise, fall away. We know that the body is subject to decay, that there is old age and death, but this is not the wisdom which can directly realize the momentary breaking up of the units which constitute the body. We do not notice their vanishing after they have arisen because there are new bodily phenomena replacing the ones that have fallen away. We can notice that there is sometimes heat in the body, sometimes cold, sometimes suppleness, sometimes stiffness. This shows that there is change of bodily phenomena. Also what we call dead matter are physical phenomena which are arising and vanishing all the time. Physical phenomena arise because of conditioning factors. When we smile or cry, when we move our hand with anger or stretch out our hand in order to give, there are different bodily phenomena caused by different mental states. Bodily phenomena and also the physical phenomena outside arise because of their own conditioning factors and they have to fall away. Science also teaches the momentary change of physical phenomena, but the aim of the Buddha's teachings is completely different, the aim is detachment from all phenomena. The "eye of wisdom" which sees impermanence is different from a microscope through which one watches the change of the smallest physical units. The wisdom which directly realizes the momentary impermanence of phenomena eventually leads to detachment.

Our life can be compared with the flux of a river. A river seems to keep its identity but in reality not one drop of water stays the same while the river is flowing on and on. In the same way what we call a "person" seems to keep its identity, but in reality there are mere passing mental phenomena and physical phenomena. These phenomena arise because of their appropriate conditions and then fall away. It can be noticed that people have different characters, but what is called "character" are phenomena which have been conditioned by phenomena in the past. Since our life is an unbroken series of moments of consciousness arising in succession, the past moments can condition the present moment and the present moment can condition the future moments. There were wholesome and unwholesome moments in the past and these condition the arising of wholesome and unwholesome moments today. What is learnt today is never lost, moments of understanding today can be accumulated and in that way understanding can develop.

We conceive life as a long duration of time, lasting from the moment of birth until death. If the momentary arising and vanishing of each reality is taken into consideration, it can be said that there is birth and death at each moment. Seeing arises but it does not last, it falls away immediately. At another moment there is hearing, but it does not last either. Thinking changes each moment, there is thinking of different things all the time. It can be noticed that there can only be thinking of one thing, not more than one thing, at a time. It may seem that thinking can last, but in reality there are different moments of consciousness succeeding one another extremely rapidly. Feelings change, there is pleasant feeling at one moment, at another moment there is unpleasant feeling and at another moment again indifferent feeling. The Buddha taught that what is impermanent is suffering, in Pāli **dukkha**[3]. Bodily pain and mental suffering due to the changeability of things are forms of dukkha which are more obvious. The truth of dukkha, however, comprises more than that. The truth of dukkha pertains to all physical phenomena and mental states which are impermanent. They are unsatisfactory because, after they have arisen, they are there merely for an extremely short moment and then they disappear completely. The truth of dukkha is deep and difficult to understand.

We read in the *Kindred Sayings* (V, Mahā-vagga, Book XII, Kindred Sayings about the Truths, Chapter 2, §1) that the Buddha, after his enlightenment, when he was staying in the Deerpark at Isipatana, near Varanasī, preached to a group of five monks. He explained to them the four noble Truths: the Truth of dukkha, the Truth of the origin of dukkha, the Truth of the ceasing of dukkha, which is nibbāna, and the Truth of the Path leading to the ceasing of dukkha. We read with regard to dukkha:

> Birth is dukkha, decay is dukkha, death is dukkha; likewise sorrow and grief, woe, lamentation and despair. To be conjoined with what we dislike; to be separated from what we like,—that also is dukkha. Not to get what one wants,—that also is dukkha. In short, these five groups of attachment are dukkha.

---

[3] The Pāli term dukkha is to be preferred, since the word "suffering" does not cover completely the meaning of the first noble Truth.

The five groups (in Pāli khandhas) of attachment are all physical phenomena and mental phenomena of our life which have been classified as five groups. They are: the group of physical phenomena, and four groups of mental phenomena comprising: the group of feelings, of perceptions, of mental activities (including all wholesome and unwholesome qualities) and of consciousness. These five groups comprise all phenomena of life which arise because of their own conditions and then fall away. Seeing is dukkha, because it arises and falls away. Colour is dukkha, pleasant feeling is dukkha, even wholesome mental states are dukkha, they all are impermanent.

There may be theoretical understanding of the fact that all that can be experienced is impermanent and therefore unsatisfactory or dukkha. The Truth of dukkha, however, cannot be realized through theoretical understanding alone. There can be thinking of the impermanence of everything in life, but it is extremely difficult to realize through one's own experience the arising and falling away, thus, the breaking up from moment to moment of phenomena. Through the development of the eightfold Path there can eventually be direct understanding of the impermanence of the phenomena of life and of their nature of dukkha.

All phenomena are impermanent. There should be precise understanding of what that "all" is. Otherwise there cannot be the realization of impermanence and dukkha. We read in the *Kindred Sayings* (IV, Kindred Sayings on Sense, First Fifty, Chapter 3, §23, The all) that the Buddha said to the monks while he was at Savatthī:

> Monks, I will teach you the all. Do you listen to it.
> And what, monks, is the all? It is eye and visible object, ear and sound, nose and scent, tongue and savour, body and tangible object, mind and mind-states. That, monks, is called the "all".

> *Whoso, monks, should say: "Rejecting this all, I will proclaim another all,—it would be mere talk on his part, and when questioned he could not make good his boast, and further would come to an ill pass. Why so? Because, monks, it would be beyond his scope to do so.*

From this sutta we see that the Buddha's teaching is very concrete, that it pertains to all realities of daily life:

> *the seeing of visible object through the eyes;*
> *the hearing of sound through the ears;*
> *the smelling of odours through the nose;*
> *the tasting of flavours through the tongue;*
> *the experience of tangible object through the body-sense;*
> *the experience of mental objects through the mind.*

When one first comes into contact with the Buddhist teachings one may be surprised that the Buddha speaks time and again about realities such as seeing and hearing. However, the "all" has to be known and investigated. There is such a great deal of ignorance of mental phenomena and physical phenomena. Generally one is inclined to be absorbed in thinking about people one saw or words one heard; one never paid attention to seeing itself or hearing itself. One may even doubt whether it is useful to do so. Seeing and hearing themselves are neither wholesome nor unwholesome, but immediately after seeing and hearing all kinds of defilements are bound to arise. All the different moments of life should be investigated thoroughly, so that there can be elimination of delusion about them.

There are different degrees of understanding realities. Thinking about realities and about their impermanence is theoretical understanding and this is not the realization of the true nature of realities. Theoretical understanding, however, can be the foundation for direct understanding of the realities which appear in daily life.

As we study the Buddhist scriptures we will learn about the realities which are to be understood. There are three parts or "baskets" of the Buddha's teachings: the Vinaya, the Suttanta or Discourses and the Abhidhamma or "higher teachings". The Vinaya is the "Book of Discipline" for the monks. The Suttanta are discourses of the Buddha held at different places to different people. The Abhidhamma is a detailed exposition of all mental phenomena and physical phenomena and also of their conditioning factors and their different ways of conditional relations. Although these three parts of the teachings are different in form, they point to the same goal: the eradication of defilements through the direct realization of the truth. When one studies the different realities which are explained in detail in the Abhidhamma, the goal should not be forgotten: the development of direct understanding of realities when they appear. There is also Abhidhamma in the suttas. The sutta about the "All" I quoted above is an example of this. The deep meaning of the suttas cannot be understood without a basic study of the Abhidhamma. The field of the Abhidhamma is immense and we cannot grasp the whole contents. However, when one begins to study it, at least in part, one will see that it can be of great assistance for the understanding of our life. Some people have doubt as to the authenticity of the Abhidhamma, they doubt whether it is the teaching of the Buddha himself. As one studies the Abhidhamma one will see for oneself that the Abhidhamma teaches about phenomena which can be experienced at this moment. The Abhidhamma deals with seeing, visible object, with all experiences through the senses and the mind, with all wholesome qualities, with all defilements. The different parts of the scriptures are one, they are the Buddha's teachings.

We read in the *Kindred Sayings* (IV, Kindred Sayings on

Sense, Second Fifty, Chapter I, §53, Ignorance) about the elimination of ignorance. We read about a conversation of a monk with the Buddha about this subject:

"By how knowing, lord, by how seeing does ignorance vanish and knowledge arise?"
"In him that knows and sees the eye as impermanent, monk, ignorance vanishes and knowledge arises. In him that knows and sees visible objects...seeing-consciousness...eye-contact...the pleasant, unpleasant or neutral feeling arising dependant on eye-contact as impermanent, monk, ignorance vanishes and knowledge arises..."

The same is said about the realities pertaining to the ear, the nose, the tongue, the body-sense and the mind. All these phenomena have to be investigated in order to know them as they are.

There is seeing, and shortly after that there is attachment to what is seen but most of the time there is ignorance of these phenomena. Even when there is no pleasant feeling on account of what is seen there can still be clinging. There is clinging time and again to seeing, to visible object, to hearing, to sound, to all that can be experienced. We would not like to be without eye-sense or ear-sense and this shows that there is clinging. We want to continue seeing, hearing and experiencing all the objects which present themselves through the senses. What is seen and what is experienced through the other senses falls away immediately, but we erroneously believe that things last, at least for a while. Because of our delusion we keep on clinging. When we do not get what we want, when we lose people who are dear to us, or things we possess, we are sad or even in despair. It is attachment which conditions aversion or sadness. When we do not get what we like there is dislike. All such mental states are realities of daily life and, instead of suppressing them, they can be investigated when they appear. Then their different characteristics can be distinguished.

Each phenomenon has a different characteristic and it arises because of different conditions. For example, when we are in the company of relatives or friends, we can notice that there are different moments of consciousness. There are moments of attachment, moments that there is clinging to our own pleasant feeling on account of the company of dear people. It may seem that we think of other people's happiness, but we are merely attached to our own happiness. There are other moments, however, that we sincerely think of the other people's wellbeing and happiness, that we do not think of ourselves. Attachment and unselfish kindness have different characteristics and gradually their difference can be learnt when they appear. It may seem complicated to analyse one's mental states. One can, however, lead one's life naturally, one can enjoy all the pleasant things of life, and at the same time develop more understanding of different moments of consciousness which arise, be it clinging, unselfish kindness or generosity. In that way there can be a more precise understanding of the different characteristics of phenomena.

When one begins to investigate the different phenomena of one's life, one realizes that there is such an amount of ignorance. It is beneficial to realize this, because that is the beginning of understanding. There is ignorance of realities such as seeing, hearing or thinking. It is not known precisely when there is seeing and when there is attachment to what is seen. Realities arise and fall away very rapidly. There is clinging to the objects which are experienced and their arising and falling away is not realized. There is ignorance of the suffering and the unsatisfactoriness inherent in all conditioned realities. Ignorance and clinging are the conditions for rebirth into a new existence, for continuation in the cycle of birth and death. When there is rebirth, there is suffering again, there will again be old age, sickness and death.

It is difficult to grasp the truth of dukkha, but one can begin to develop more understanding of the phenomena which appear in one's life. The Buddha taught Dhamma in order that people could investigate all realities. The word "dhamma" has different meanings, but in its widest sense dhamma is everything which is real and which has its own characteristic. Seeing is dhamma, attachment is dhamma, anger is dhamma. They are realities which can be experienced by everybody. We can read about seeing, attachment or anger, but when these realities occur we can learn to distinguish their different characteristics. Knowledge of realities can be acquired through the study of the Abhidhamma, but this knowledge should be applied so that there can eventually be direct understanding of realities. We are full of attachment, anger, avarice, conceit, jealousy, full of defilements, but understanding of all these realities can be developed. If dislike, for example, would be suppressed, instead of knowing its characteristic when it appears, there would be ignorance of the way it is conditioned. It would not be known that it is attachment which conditions dislike. If there is ignorance of what is wholesome and what is unwholesome, wholesome qualities could not be developed. Understanding can be developed of the countless moments of attachment which arise after seeing, hearing and the other experiences through the senses. All realities arise because of their own conditions.

The development of direct understanding of realities is the Path leading to the end of dukkha. The development of this Path is very gradual and takes a long time. The characteristics of the different realities which appear have to be thoroughly investigated and understood. In that way it can be gradually seen that they arise each because of their own conditions. What arises because of conditions has to fall away, it is impermanent. The impermanence of realities, their momentary breaking up, can only be realized at a later stage of the development of understanding. Eventually there can be the realization of the fact that all conditioned realities which arise and fall away are dukkha. There are different degrees of understanding the Truth of dukkha. When one attains enlightenment one has understood the Truth of dukkha, of the origin of dukkha, of the ceasing of dukkha and of the way leading to the ceasing of dukkha.

Chapter 3

The truth of non-self

All phenomena of life are impermanent and dukkha. Seeing, colour, hearing, sound, feeling, anger, greed or generosity, arise because of their own conditions and then they fall away immediately. There is no abiding ego or "self" who could cause the arising of these phenomena or exert control over them. Realities which are impermanent and dukkha are non-self. We read in the *Kindred Sayings* (IV, Kindred Sayings on Sense, First Fifty, Chapter 1, §1, impermanent, the personal) that the Buddha, while staying at the Jeta Grove near Savatthī, said to the monks:

> *The eye, monks, is impermanent. What is impermanent, that is dukkha. What is dukkha, that is void of the self. What is void of the self, that is not mine; I am not it; it is not my self. That is how it is to be regarded with perfect insight of what it really is.*
>
> *The ear is impermanent...The nose is impermanent...The tongue is impermanent...The body is impermanent...The mind is impermanent. What is impermanent, that is dukkha. What is dukkha, that is void of the self. What is void of the self, that is not mine; I am not it; it is not my self. That is how it is to be regarded with perfect insight of what it really is....*

We then read that through insight all clinging to the senses and the mind is eradicated and that there are consequently no more conditions for rebirth. In the following suttas the same is said with regard to colour, sound, scent, savour, tangible object and mind-object. They are impermanent, dukkha and void of the self.

The truth of non-self, in Pāli **anattā**, is an essential element of the Buddha's teachings. This truth has been taught by the Buddha alone, it cannot be found outside the Buddhist teachings. Those who come into contact with Buddhism for the first time may be bewildered, even repelled by the truth of non-self. They wonder what the world would be without a self, without other people. Do we not live with and for other people? It is difficult to grasp the truth of non-self and its implications in daily life.

What is called in conventional language a "person" or "self" is merely a temporary combination of physical phenomena and mental phenomena, which are depending on each other. They have been classified as five groups, in Pāli khandhas: one group of all physical phenomena and four groups of mental phenomena—feelings, perceptions, mental activities and consciousness. The five khandhas are in a flux, in a constant process of formation and dissolution. There is nothing lasting, nothing eternal, nothing unchanging in life.

The khandhas which arise, fall away and do not return. Present khandhas are different from past khandhas but they are conditioned by past khandhas, and present khandhas condition in their turn future khandhas. We read in the *Dialogues of the Buddha* (I, number IX, Potthapāda Sutta) that the Buddha explained to Citta about the three modes of personality: the past, the present and the future personality. They are different, but the past conditions the present and the present conditions the future. We read that the Buddha explained this by way of a simile:

> *Just, Citta, as from a cow comes milk, and from the milk curds, and from the curds butter, and from the butter ghee, and from the ghee junket; but when it is milk it is not called curds, or butter, or ghee, or*

junket; and when it is curds it is not called by any of the other names...

Just so, Citta, when any one of the three modes of personality is going on, it is not called by the name of the other. For these, Citta, are merely names, expressions, turns of speech, designations in common use in the world. And of these a Tathāgata[4] makes use indeed, but is not led astray by them.

We call by such or such a name what are actually the five khandhas. People have different characters, different personalities. In reality there is nothing static in what is called a person. The present personality is different from the past personality, but it has originated from the past personality. We read in the commentary to the *Debates* (to the *Kathāvatthu*, Chapter I, the Person):

...Given bodily and mental khandhas, it is customary to say such and such a name, a family. Thus, by this popular turn of speech, convention, expression, is meant: "there is the person"...The Buddhas have two kinds of discourse, the popular and the philosophical. Those relating to a being, a person, a deva (divine being), a "brahmā",...are popular discourses, while those relating to impermanence, dukkha, non-self, the khandhas, the elements, the senses...are discourses on ultimate meaning...A discourse on ultimate meaning is, as a rule, too severe to begin with; therefore the Buddhas teach at first by popular discourse, and then by way of discourse on ultimate meaning...

The Enlightened One, best of speakers, spoke two kinds of truth, namely, the conventional truth and the ultimate truth, a third is not known.

Therein, a popular discourse is true in conventional sense. A discourse on ultimate realities is also true, and as such, characteristic of things as they are...

---

[4] Literally, "Thus-gone", epithet of the Buddha.

Before studying the Buddhist teachings we only knew conventional truth: the truth of the world populated by people and animals, the world of persons, of self. Through the Buddhist teachings we learn about the ultimate truth: the mental phenomena and physical phenomena which are impermanent.

The truth of non-self is ultimate truth. It is deep and hard to penetrate. It has been taught by way of similes in the Buddhist scriptures and in the commentaries. The great commentator Buddhaghosa, in his book the *Path of Purification* (Visuddhimagga), illustrates the truth of non-self with similes from Buddhist scriptures. The *Path of Purification* is a comprehensive exposition of the Buddha's teaching based on old commentaries and the tradition of the monks in Sri Lanka, written in the fifth century A.D. Buddhaghosa explains that when one thinks of a whole of mind and body, one clings to the concept of person, whereas when this "whole" is seen as different elements which are impermanent, one will lose the perception of "self":

We read in the *Path of Purification* (XVIII, 25, 26):

> *As with the assembly of parts*
> *The word "chariot" is countenanced,*
> *So, when the khandhas are present,*
> *"A being" is said in common usage*[5].

> *Again, this has been said: "Just as when a space is enclosed with timber and creepers and grass and clay, there comes to be the term 'house', so too, when a space is enclosed with bones and sinews and flesh and skin, there comes to be the term 'material form'*[6]*."*

---

[5] see Kindred Sayings I, 135

[6] see Middle Length Sayings I, number 28

Further on (XVIII, 28) we read:

> So in many hundred suttas it is only mentality-materiality that is illustrated, not a being, not a person. Therefore, just as when the component parts such as axles, wheels, frame, poles, etc. are arranged in a certain way, there comes to be the mere term of common usage "chariot", yet in the ultimate sense when each part is examined, there is no chariot—and just as when the component parts of a house such as wattles, etc. are placed so that they enclose a space in a certain way, there comes to be the mere term of common usage "house", yet in the ultimate sense there is no house,... so too, when there are the five khandhas of clinging, there comes to be the mere term of common usage "a being", "a person", yet in the ultimate sense, when each component is examined, there is no being as a basis for the assumption "I am" or "I"; in the ultimate sense there is only mentality-materiality. The vision of one who sees in this way is called right vision.

If life can be considered as existing in just one moment, it will be less difficult to understand the truth of non-self. In the *Mahā-Niddesa* (number 6, Decay) the Buddha explains that life is extremely short. In the ultimate sense it lasts only as long as one moment of consciousness. Each moment of consciousness which arises falls away completely, to be succeeded by the next moment which is different.

We read in the *Path of Purification* (XX, 72) a quotation from the *Mahā-Niddesa* text about the khandhas which are impermanent:

> No store of broken states, no future stock;
> Those born balance like seeds on needle points.
> Break-up of states is fore-doomed at their birth;
> Those present decay, unmingled with those past.

They come from nowhere, break up, nowhere go;
Flash in and out, as lightning in the sky.

One is used to thinking of a self who coordinates all the different experiences through the senses and the mind, a self who can see, hear and think all at the same time, but in reality there can be only one moment of consciousness at a time which experiences one object. At one moment life is seeing, at another moment life is hearing and at another moment again life is thinking. Each moment of our life arises because of its own conditions, exists for an extremely short time and then falls away. Seeing arises dependant on eye-sense, on colour and on other factors. It exists just for a moment and then it is gone. Seeing arises and falls away very rapidly, but then there are other moments of seeing again and this causes us to erroneously believe that seeing lasts. The seeing of this moment, however, is different from seeing which is just past. Colour which appears at this moment is different from colour which is just past. How could there be a self who exerts control over seeing or any other reality? Realities such as kindness and anger arise because of their own conditions, there is no self who could exert control over them. We would like to speak kindly, but when there are conditions for anger, it arises. We may tell ourselves to keep silent, but, before we realize it, angry words have been spoken already. There was anger in the past and this has been accumulated. That is why it can arise at any time. Anger does not belong to a person, but it is a reality. We are used to identifying ourselves with realities such as anger, generosity, seeing or thinking, but it can be learnt that they are mental phenomena, arising because of their own conditions. We are used to identifying ourselves with our body, but the body consists of changing physical phenomena, arising because of their own conditions. Bodily phenomena are beyond control; ageing, sickness and death cannot be prevented. Realities come and go very rapidly, they can be compared with a flash of lightning. One cannot exercise any power over a flash of lightning, it is gone as soon as it has been noticed. Evenso, one cannot exert control over the mental and physical phenomena of one's life.

The outer appearance of things deludes us as to what is really there: fleeting phenomena which are beyond control. We read in the commentary to the *Dhammapada* (Buddhist Legends II, Book IV, 2) about a monk who meditated on a mirage, but was unable to reach the state of perfection. He decided to visit the Buddha and on his way he saw a mirage. We read that he said to himself: "Even as this mirage seen in the season of the heat appears substantial to those who are far off, but vanishes on nearer approach, so also is this existence unsubstantial by reason of birth and decay."

We read that he meditated on this mirage. Wearied from his journey he bathed in the river Aciravatī and then sat near a waterfall:

> ...As he sat there watching great bubbles of foam rising and bursting, from the force of the water striking against the rocks, he said to himself, "Just so is this existence also produced and just so does it burst." And this he took for his subject of meditation.
>
> The Teacher, seated in his perfumed chamber, saw the Elder and said, "Monk, it is even so. Like a bubble of foam or a mirage is this existence. Precisely thus is it produced and precisely thus does it pass away." And when he had thus spoken, he pronounced the following stanza:
>
> "He who knows that this body is like foam, he who clearly comprehends that it is of the nature of a mirage,

> *Such a man will break the flower-tipped arrows of Māra and will go where the King of Death will not see him."*

We read that the monk at the conclusion of this stanza reached the state of perfection. Māra represents all that is evil, he is the King of Death. The person who has eradicated all defilements will not be reborn, there will not be for him anymore old age, sickness and death, thus, the "King of Death" will not see him anymore.

Life is like a mirage, we are time and again deceived and tricked by the outer appearance of things. We believe that what we experience can last, at least for a while, and that there is a self who experiences things, a lasting personality. We take our wrong perceptions to be true, we have a distorted view of realities. Through the development of precise understanding of different realities which appear one at a time, our distorted view can be corrected.

It is difficult to understand and accept that whatever arises does so because of its own conditions and that it is beyond control. People generally want to control their lives, to take their destinies in their own hands. It can, however, even on the theoretical level, be understood that it is impossible to control one's life. One cannot control one's body, one cannot control the different moments of consciousness which arise. When there is, for example, the tasting of a delicious sweet, there is bound to be clinging to the flavour immediately after having tasted it. Tasting arises dependent on tasting-sense, on flavour which impinges on tasting-sense and on other conditions; clinging to the flavour arises because of its own conditions, because of the accumulation of the tendency to clinging. Different moments of consciousness succeed one another so rapidly that it seems that several of them can occur at the same time. So long as there is no precise understanding they cannot be distinguished from each other. In reality only one moment of consciousness can arise at a time. I will give an example of different moments of consciousness, arising each because of their own conditions. Someone had given me a huge teddybear which I put in a chair. Time and again it happened that when I walked past it at dusk there were moments of fear before I realized that it was a teddybear. There was seeing which experienced colour or visible object impinging on the eye-sense, and then, before knowing that there was a teddybear, there were many other moments of consciousness. There can be fear on account of what is seen, before it is known that it is a harmless object. There were moments of recognizing and defining and when there was the registration that there was only a toy, the fear was gone. This example illustrates that there are different conditions for the different moments of consciousness which arise. They arise each because of their own conditions and in a particular order. They arise and fall away so rapidly that there would not even be time to control or direct them. There is no mind, no soul which lasts, merely rapidly changing moments of consciousness.

It is inevitable that questions arise with regard to the implication of the truth of non-self in one's life. People generally have questions as to the existence of a free will. If there is no self, only empty phenomena which appear and disappear, can there be a free will, can one have a free choice in the taking of decisions in life? Are a free will and self-control not essential elements of human life? The truth of non-self seems to imply that one's whole life is determined, even predestined, by conditions. The answer is that a free will presupposes a lasting personality who can exert power over his will. Since there is no "self", merely impermanent phenomena arising because of conditions, there is no free will independent of conditions. The will or desire to act can be wholesome at one moment and unwholesome at another moment. When there is anger, there is volition which is unwholesome, and it can instigate words of anger. When there is generosity, there is volition which is wholesome, it can motivate deeds of generosity. There can be the decision to do particular things, such as the development of generosity or of understanding, but there is no person who decides to do this. There are different moments of decision arising because of different conditions. What one decides to do depends on past accumulations of wholesomeness and unwholesomeness, on one's education, on the friends one associates with. It may be felt that, since accumulations of wholesomeness and unwholesomeness in the past condition one's actions, speech and thoughts today, one would be a helpless victim of these accumulated conditions. What is the sense of life if everything is determined. So long as there is clinging to a concept of self there is enslavement, no freedom. When understanding is developed which can eliminate the clinging to a self one becomes really free. Also the development of understanding is conditioned, it is conditioned by moments of understanding in the past, by association with someone who can explain the Dhamma, by the study of the Buddhist teachings. Whatever we think or do is dependent on conditions which operate in our life in an intricate way. The fifth book of the Abhidhamma deals entirely with the different conditions for on all mental and physical phenomena of life, with the aim to help people to have more understanding of these conditions. Even freedom is dependent on conditions. The more understanding of realities develops, the more will there be the letting go of clinging to the importance of self, the clinging to wrong perceptions of reality. Eventually all defilements can be eradicated by right understanding and is this not what can be called the highest freedom?

In order to be able to understand the truth of non-self, the difference has to be known between what is real in the ultimate sense and what is real in conventional sense. It is difficult to clearly know the difference and I will deal with this subject again later on. Seeing, hearing, colour, sound or thinking are real in the ultimate sense. This does not mean that they are abstract categories. They have each their own characteristic and they can be directly experienced. Seeing, for example has a characteristic which is different from the characteristic of hearing. These characteristics do not change, they are the same for everybody. Seeing is always seeing, hearing is always hearing, no matter how one names them. Concepts or ideas such as person, world, animal, are conventional realities one can think of, but they are not real in the ultimate sense. They have no characteristics which can be directly experienced. It is not wrong to think of concepts such as persons, but it is not in conformity with reality to ascribe properties to them which they do not have, such as permanence and substantiality. We delude ourselves if we take our wrong perceptions to be true. It is essential to learn the difference between realities and concepts, otherwise there cannot be the development of the Buddha's Path.

So long as understanding has not been developed to the stage that the momentary breaking up of physical phenomena and mental phenomena has been realized, it is impossible to see things as they really are. We believe that seeing lasts for a while and that what is seen also lasts. Our world seems to be full of people, we believe that we really see them. In reality seeing doesn't last and colour which is seen doesn't last either. When we "see" people the situation is the same as watching the projected images on a screen which are rapidly changing. We "see" the image of a person or a thing, but the outer appearance is misleading. In reality there are many different moments arising and falling away, succeeding one another. There are processes of seeing, recognizing, classifying, defining and thinking. When it seems that we see a "whole", the image of a person, it is actually thinking which is conditioned by seeing, by the experience of what is visible.

The Buddha spoke about all that can be experienced through the senses and through the mind in order to help people to develop understanding of realities and to know the truth about them, to realize them as impermanent, dukkha and not self. Seeing is a reality, but it is not self, hearing is a reality, but it is not self, thinking is a reality, but it is not self.

A question which may arise is the following: if people do not exist, what is the sense of developing kindness, which has to be directed towards people, what is the sense of committing oneself to the improvement of the world? The answer is that knowing the truth about realities is no impediment to deal with people, to perform deeds of kindness and to commit oneself to the improvement of the world. Buddhism does not propagate a passive attitude towards the world, on the contrary, it promotes the performing of one's tasks with more unselfishness, with more wholesomeness. We usually think of people in an unwholesome way, with clinging, aversion and delusion. We cling to an image of ourselves and also to images of other people. We have an image of how they should behave towards us. When someone else does not conform to the image we have of him we are disappointed or even angry. Clinging to images we form up conditions many kinds of defilements, such as conceit, jealousy, avarice or possessiveness. Through the Buddhist teachings we can learn to think of people in the right way, that is, without clinging to false images. While we are in the company of people and talk to them there can be the development of understanding of realities which appear through the senses and the mind. The realisation of the truth that there is no lasting person or self, merely fleeting phenomena, does not mean that one has to shun one's task in society. The Buddha himself was caring for other people, he was thinking of his disciples, he was intent on the welfare of all beings, but he had no wrong view of an abiding person, of a self. He was an example of kindness, patience and compassion. He visited sick monks and looked after them, he preached Dhamma for forty-five years. He exhorted people to develop kindness and compassion towards other beings. Even when one has realized the truth of non-self one can still think of beings, but instead of thinking with clinging, with selfishness, there are conditions to think more often in the wholesome way, and this is to the benefit of oneself and others.

There is no lasting substance or self in the combination of fleeting physical phenomena and mental phenomena we call "person". Neither is there a "higher self" outside. Some people believe that what we could call a self will after death be dissolved into a "higher self" into the "All", or the cosmos. This is not the Buddha's teaching. Even nibbāna, the unconditioned reality, is not self. All conditioned phenomena of life are impermanent, dukkha and not self. The unconditioned reality, nibbāna, does not have the characteristics of impermanence and dukkha, but it does have the characteristic of non-self.

We read in the *Dhammapada* (verse 277-279):

All conditioned realities are impermanent.
Who perceives this fact with wisdom,

*Straightaway becomes contemptuous of suffering.
This is the Path to Purity.*

*All conditioned realities are dukkha.
Who perceives this fact with wisdom,
Straightaway becomes contemptuous of suffering.
This is the Path to Purity.*

*All dhammas are non-self.
Who perceives this fact with wisdom,
Straightaway becomes contemptuous of suffering.
This is the Path to Purity.*

The text states that all dhammas are non-self. Nibbāna is not a conditioned reality, but it is real, it is dhamma. Therefore the text states that all dhammas, including nibbāna, are non-self.

The development of the eightfold Path is in fact the development of understanding of ultimate realities: of seeing, colour, hearing, sound, of all that can be experienced through the senses and the mind. The reader may find it monotonous to read in the texts of the scriptures time and again about these realities. The aim of the teaching on ultimate realities, however, is the eradication of the concept of self. The clinging to the concept of self has to be eradicated first before there can be the elimination of other defilements. When a person can be seen as five khandhas, mere elements, which are arising and vanishing, there are conditions for being less inclined to attachment and aversion towards the vicissitudes of life, such as praise and blame, gain and loss, which play such an important role in our life. We read in "The Simile of the Elephant's Footprint" (Middle Length Sayings I, number 28) that the Buddha's disciple Sāriputta explained to the monks realities by way of elements. He explained that the body should not be seen as "I", "mine", or "I am". We read:

> ...Your reverences, if others abuse, revile, annoy, vex this monk, he comprehends: "This painful feeling that has arisen in me is born of sensory impingement on the ear, it has a cause, it is not without a cause. What is the cause? Sensory impingement is the cause." He sees that sensory impingement is impermanent, he sees that feeling... perception...mental activities are impermanent, he sees that consciousness is impermanent. His mind rejoices, is pleased, composed and is set on the objects of the element...

We are inclined to blame other people when they speak in a disagreeable way, instead of realizing that there is merely sound impinging on the ear-sense, elements impinging on elements. So long as there is clinging to a self realities cannot be seen as mere elements. This sutta makes clear that it is beneficial to understand the truth of non-self. It can only be realized very gradually, in developing understanding of the realities included in the five khandhas.

Chapter 4

The mind

The Buddha taught the truth of non-self. What is called the mind or the soul is not a self, but ever-changing mental elements which are arising and falling away. The implication of this truth is difficult to grasp. Before coming into contact with Buddhism we considered the mind to be the core and essence of the human personality. We considered the mind as that which thinks, takes decisions and charts the course of our life. In order to understand the Buddha's teaching on the mind as non-self, it is necessary to have a more detailed knowledge of the mind. The word mind is misleading since it is associated with particular concepts of Western philosophy, it is usually associated merely with thinking. The mind according to the Buddhist teaching experiences or cognizes an object, and this has to be taken in its widest sense. I prefer therefore to use the Pāli term citta (pronounced "chitta"). Citta is derived from the Pāli term "cinteti", being aware or thinking. Citta is conscious or aware of an object.

"Mind", "soul" or "spirit" are "conventional realities". Through the Buddhist teachings we learn about ultimate realities as I explained in the preceding chapter. All mental activities we used to ascribe to "our mind" are carried out by citta, not by one citta, but by many different cittas. Cittas are moments of consciousness which are impermanent, they are arising and falling away, succeeding one another. Our life is an unbroken series of cittas. If there were no citta, we would not be alive, we could not think, read, study, act or speak. When we walk or when we stretch out our hand to take hold of something, it is citta which conditions our movements. It is citta which perceives the world outside; if there were no citta nothing could appear. The world outside appears through eyes, ears, nose, tongue, body-sense and mind. We think of what is seen, heard or experienced through the other senses. There are not merely cittas which think, the cittas which think are alternated with cittas which see, hear or experience objects through the other senses. When we touch something which is hard or soft, there are cittas which experience tangible object through the body-sense, and then there are cittas which think of what was touched, a table or a chair.

Before we studied the Buddhist teachings we did not consider the mind as a reality which can see or hear. The Buddha taught that also seeing and hearing are cittas. There is a great variety of cittas which each experience an object. The citta which sees, seeing-consciousness, experiences an object: visible object or colour. It experiences visible object through the eye-sense. Eye-sense is the "doorway" through which seeing-consciousness experiences visible object. Hearing-consciousness experiences sound through the doorway of the ear-sense. Seeing and hearing are entirely different cittas which are depending on different conditions. Cittas experience objects through the doorways of eye, ear, nose, tongue, body-sense and mind. Before studying the Buddhist teachings we did not pay attention to seeing as being a citta experiencing visible object through the eye-door, or to hearing as being a citta experiencing sound through the ear-door. Cittas, objects and doorways are ultimate realities taught by the Buddha.

One may doubt the usefulness of knowing details on cittas, objects and doorways. It is important to know more thoroughly the phenomena of our life which are occurring

Chapter 4 • The mind

all the time. We are deluded as to the truth when we believe that they are lasting and that they are "self", or belonging to a "self", that we can exert control over them. The Buddha taught that they are impermanent, dukkha and non-self. These characteristics are not abstract categories, they pertain to seeing, eye-sense, visible object, to all phenomena which are arising and falling away from moment to moment. Since understanding of the truth of these phenomena can only gradually develop, we should begin to investigate them more closely. In the ultimate sense there are merely mental phenomena and physical phenomena. So long as they cannot be distinguished from each other, there cannot be a precise knowledge of them.

The citta which sees, seeing-consciousness, is a mental phenomenon, it experiences an object. It is dependent on eye-sense, which is a physical phenomenon. Eye-sense does not see but it has the quality of receiving colour, so that seeing-consciousness can experience that colour. Colour or visible object is also a physical phenomenon, it cannot experience anything. Seeing, hearing and the experiences through the other senses are dependent on conditions. If there were no doorways the different sense objects could not be experienced, and consequently what we call "the world outside" could not appear. When we are fast asleep, without dreaming, the world does not appear. We do not know who our parents or friends are, we do not know the place where we are living. When we wake up the world around us appears again. We can verify that there is impingement of the sense objects on the appropriate senses and this is the condition for the experience of the world around us. There are cittas which see, hear and experience the other sense objects, and these experiences condition thinking about the world of people and things. We are usually absorbed in our thoughts concerning the people and things around us and we do not realize that it is citta which thinks. We could not think of "self", person or possessions, which are conventional realities, if there were not the ultimate realities of colour, sound and the other sense objects and the cittas which experience them through the appropriate doorways.

There can be merely one citta at a time, experiencing one object. It seems that several cittas can occur at the same time, but in reality this is not so. Different cittas, such as seeing and hearing, experience different objects and are dependent on different doorways. Seeing, hearing and thinking are different cittas arising at different moments. We can notice that seeing is not hearing, that they are different experiences. If they would occur at the same time we would not be able to know that they are different. Cittas arise and fall away very rapidly; the citta which has fallen away is immediately succeeded by the next citta. It seems that seeing, hearing or thinking can last for a while, but in reality they exist merely for an extremely short moment.

There is a great variety of cittas which arise because of their appropriate conditions. There are cittas which see, hear, experience objects through the other senses and think about these objects. The cittas which see, hear, smell, taste or experience an object through the body-sense neither like nor dislike the object, they do not react to the object in an unwholesome or a wholesome way. These types of citta are neither kusala nor akusala. However, shortly after they have fallen away there are cittas which are not neutral, but which react to the objects experienced through the senses either in an unwholesome way or in a wholesome way. Thus, there are kusala cittas, there are akusala cittas, and there are cittas which are neither kusala nor akusala. Time and again there is seeing or hearing and on account of the object which is experienced there are cittas which are either kusala or akusala. When there is thinking, there is either kusala citta or akusala citta. There are also cittas which motivate good or bad actions and speech. When we give a present there are wholesome cittas, kusala cittas with generosity which motivate our giving. When we speak harsh words, there are unwholesome cittas, akusala cittas with anger which motivate our speech.

Different inclinations to kusala and akusala have been accumulated. Accumulated tendencies are like microbes, they are lying dormant, but they can appear at any time when there is an opportunity for them to appear. In this connection the term "subconsciousness" is used in Western psychology, designating that part of the mind which is not ordinarily known, but which shows itself for example in dreams. The term subconsciousness is misleading, it implies something static. In reality there are accumulated tendencies, but they are not static, they are accumulating from moment to moment; they are conditions for the arising of kusala citta or akusala citta later on. At each moment of kusala citta or akusala citta the process of accumulation continues; kusala citta and akusala citta arising today are conditions for the arising of kusala citta and akusala citta in the future. Each citta which arises falls away, but since it is succeeded by the next citta without any interval, the process of accumulation can go on from moment to moment.

There are different types of kusala citta and of akusala citta. It is important to learn more about them in order to understand ourselves, the way we behave towards others in action and speech, and the way we react towards pleasant and unpleasant events. It is citta which motivates good deeds and evil deeds. We read in the *Middle Length*

Sayings (II, number 78, Discourse to Samaṇamaṇḍikā) that the Buddha explained to the carpenter Pañcakaṅga about akusala cittas and kusala cittas:

> And which, carpenter, are the unskilled moral habits? Unskilled deed of body, unskilled deed of speech, evil mode of livelihood—these, carpenter, are called unskilled moral habits. And how, carpenter, do these unskilled moral habits originate? Their origination is spoken of too. It should be answered that the origination is in the citta. Which citta? For the citta is manifold, various, diverse. That citta which has attachment, aversion, ignorance—originating from this are unskilled moral habits...

The Buddha also said of skilled moral habits that they originate from the citta, the citta which is without attachment, aversion and ignorance. Thus, all evil deeds originate from akusala citta and all wholesome deeds originate from kusala citta.

Akusala can be described as an unhealthy state of mind, as unskilled, blameworthy, faulty, unprofitable, as having unhappy results. Kusala can be described as a healthy state of mind, as skilful, faultless, profitable, as having happy results.

We read in the above quoted sutta that the citta is manifold, various, diverse. The akusala citta with attachment is quite different from kusala citta with generosity. What types of reality are attachment and generosity? Are they cittas or are they other types of reality? They are mental qualities, mental factors which can accompany citta. Attachment is an unwholesome mental quality, a defilement, whereas generosity is a wholesome mental quality. Citta can think, motivate actions or speech for example, with attachment, with anger, with generosity, with compassion. There is only one citta at a time, but it is accompanied by several mental factors or mental coadjuncts, and these condition the citta to be so various. Greed, avarice, anger, jealousy or conceit are unwholesome mental factors which can accompany akusala citta. Generosity, loving-kindness, compassion or wisdom are wholesome mental factors which can accompany kusala citta. The mental factors which accompany citta in various combinations arise and fall away together with the citta.

The commentary to the first book of the Abhidhamma, *the Expositor* (I, Part II, Chapter I, 67), uses a simile of the king and his retinue. Just as the king does not come without his attendants, the citta does not arise alone but is accompanied by several mental factors. As to the cittas which arise all the time in daily life, it can be said that citta is the chief, the principal, in knowing the object, and that the mental factors assist the citta. The citta which thinks, for example with generosity, is the chief in knowing the object, and generosity assists the citta to think in the wholesome way. The citta which thinks with jealousy is the chief in knowing the object, and jealousy assists the citta to think in the unwholesome way.

Among the unwholesome mental factors which accompany akusala citta there are three which are called "roots", namely: attachment, aversion and ignorance. Among the wholesome mental factors which accompany kusala citta there are three roots, namely: non-attachment, non-aversion and wisdom. The word "root" is used in the Buddhist teachings, since it is the firm support for the citta, being an important condition, just as the root of a tree is the firm support for the tree, the means of providing saps, necessary for its growth. The unwholesome roots of attachment, aversion and ignorance which can be associated with akusala citta have many shades and degrees; they can be coarse or more subtle. Attachment can be so strong that it motivates bad deeds such as stealing or lying, but it can also be of a more subtle degree, a degree of attachment which does not motivate any deed. Attachment can be expecting something pleasant for oneself, wishing, liking, longing, affection, self-indulgence, lust, possessiveness or covetousness. Even when we hope that other people like us, when we wish to have a good name, there are akusala cittas rooted in attachment. When we, for example, give a present to someone else there is generosity, but there can also be moments of hoping or expecting to gain something in return for our gift. Such expectations are motivated by clinging. Akusala is not the same as what is generally meant by sin or immorality. Also the more subtle degrees of attachment which do not motivate bad deeds are akusala, they are unhelpful, harmful. They are accumulated from moment to moment and thus attachment increases evermore. Clinging is deeply rooted and it is important to know our deep rooted tendencies. Affection is a form of attachment which is in society not regarded as harmful. One feels affection for parents, relatives, children or friends. It should be understood, however, that when there is affection, there is actually clinging to one's own pleasant feeling, derived from being in the company of a loved one. When there is mourning for someone who has died, there is sadness conditioned by clinging to oneself. Affection conditions fear of loss, aversion and sadness. We read in the *Kindred Sayings* (IV, Part VIII, Kindred Sayings about Headmen, §11) that the Buddha, while staying at Uruvelakappa, explained to the headman Bhadragaka that clinging is the cause of dukkha. We read that Bhadragaka said:

> *"Wonderful, lord! Strange it is, lord, how well said is this saying of the Exalted One: 'Whatsoever dukkha arising comes upon me,—all that*

is rooted in desire. Desire is indeed the root of dukkha.'
Now, lord, there is my boy,—Ciravāsi is his name. He lodges away from here. At the time of rising up, lord, I send off a man, saying: 'Go, my man, inquire of Ciravāsi.' Then, lord, till that man comes back again, I am in an anxious state, fearing lest some sickness may have befallen Ciravāsi."

"Now, what do you think, headman? Would sorrow and grief, woe, lamentation and despair come upon you if your boy Ciravāsi were slain or imprisoned or had loss or blame?"

"Lord, if such were to befall my boy Ciravāsi, how should I not have sorrow and grief, woe, lamentation and despair?"

"But, headman, you must regard it in this manner: 'Whatsoever dukkha arising comes upon me,—all that is rooted in desire, is joined to desire. Desire is indeed the root of dukkha.'"

It is impossible to be without clinging so long as the state of perfection has not been reached. We cannot force ourselves not to have clinging, but it is beneficial to realize when there is clinging, even when it is of a subtle degree, and when there is detachment. There is attachment when we like landscapes, when we enjoy shopping or talking to friends, or even when we get up in order to fetch a glass of water. Attachment can be accompanied by pleasant feeling or by indifferent feeling. When there is indifferent feeling there can still be attachment, but we may not notice it.

Aversion is another unwholesome root. Aversion dislikes the object which is experienced, whereas attachment likes it. Aversion cannot arise at the same time as attachment, but it is conditioned by it. Aversion has many shades and degrees, it can be dissatisfaction, frustration, disappointment, dejection, sadness, fear, grief, despair, revulsion, resentment, moodiness or irritability. Unpleasant feeling invariably goes together with this unwholesome root. When there is even a slight feeling of uneasiness there is citta rooted in aversion. When we have envy or stinginess there is citta rooted in aversion. In the case of envy, one dislikes it that someone else enjoys pleasant things, one wants to obtain them for oneself. In the case of avarice one does not want to share one's possessions with someone else. Aversion can also motivate killing, harsh speech rudeness or cruelty.

Another unwholesome root is ignorance. This is not the same as what is meant by ignorance in conventional language. In Buddhism ignorance has a specific meaning: it is ignorance of the characteristic of kusala and of akusala, of the truth of non-self, of the four noble Truths, in short, of ultimate realities. There are many degrees of ignorance. Ignorance is the root of all evil. Whenever there is citta rooted in attachment and citta rooted in aversion, there is also the root of ignorance. When one hears a pleasant sound, attachment is likely to arise and then there is ignorance as well. When one hears a harsh sound, aversion is likely to arise and then there is ignorance as well. Ignorance does not know the realities which arise, it does not know that attachment and aversion are akusala. Ignorance is like darkness or blindness. When there is ignorance the real nature of realities is covered up.

The three wholesome roots of non-attachment, non-aversion and wisdom have many shades and degrees. Non-attachment can be unselfishness, generosity, renunciation or dispassion. Each kusala citta is rooted in non-attachment. Whenever there is kusala citta, there is no clinging at that moment but detachment. Each kusala citta is rooted not only in non-attachment, it is also rooted in non-aversion. Non-aversion has many degrees: it can be loving-kindness, forbearance or endurance. Loving-kindness is directed towards beings, and forbearance or endurance can also pertain to situations and things. When the temperature is too hot or too cold there is bound to be dislike. When the benefit of forbearance is seen, one is not disturbed by the temperature and one does not complain. Wisdom is the third wholesome root. Wisdom does not accompany each kusala citta. Wisdom is a condition for the arising of kusala citta more often. Wisdom or understanding in Buddhism is understanding of realities. It has many degrees, it can be theoretical understanding of realities or direct understanding of the reality which appears. It can be understanding of kusala as kusala, of akusala as akusala, of good and evil deeds and their results, of the truth of non-self, of the four noble Truths. Understanding can be gradually developed. The direct understanding of realities leads to the eradication of defilements.

When there is kusala citta there are no attachment, aversion or ignorance with the citta. Kusala citta motivates wholesome deeds and speech. It depends on accumulations of kusala and akusala in the past what type of citta arises. Good friends or bad friends one associates with are also an important condition for the arising of kusala cittas or akusala cittas. When one associates with a wise friend there are conditions for the arising of kusala citta more often. There are many more akusala cittas arising than kusala cittas because of the accumulated defilements which condition them, but this is unnoticed. Just as we do not notice the amount of dirt on our hands until we wash them, evenso do we not know the amount of defilements until understanding of realities is developed.

Citta experiences pleasant and unpleasant objects through the senses and through the mind-door. When a pleasant object is experienced, attachment is likely to arise and when an unpleasant object is experienced, aversion is likely to arise. It is natural that pleasant objects are liked and unpleasant objects are disliked. It seems that we are ruled by the objects which are experienced. The pleasant object or unpleasant object is a condition for the citta which arises, but there is nothing compulsive in the nature of the object that could determine the reaction towards it. It depends on one's accumulated inclinations whether one reacts in a wholesome way or in an unwholesome way to the pleasant and unpleasant objects which are experienced through the senses and through the mind-door. After seeing, hearing or the experience of objects through the other senses there can be "unwise attention" or "wise attention" to the object. When there is unwise attention to the object, there are akusala cittas, and when there is wise attention to the object there are kusala cittas. When there is a pleasant object, there can be attachment and in that case there is unwise attention. We may, for example, only be intent on our own enjoyment of the pleasant object and not inclined to share it with others. Whereas, when there is wise attention, we are inclined to share a pleasant object with others, and then there are kusala cittas with generosity. When there is an unpleasant object, there can be aversion and thus there is unwise attention. Someone else may for example speak harsh words to us and most of the time we dislike such speech, we even blame that person for his harsh speech. Aversion, however, does not necessarily have to arise. When it is remembered that the person who speaks harshly makes himself unhappy there may be compassion instead of anger or aversion. When there is wise attention there can be forbearance and patience even when the object is unpleasant.

It is beneficial to learn more details about the many different types of citta: kusala citta, akusala citta and citta which is neither kusala nor akusala. When there is ignorance of akusala and kusala, the disadvantage of

Chapter 4 • The mind

akusala and the benefit of kusala cannot be seen. We long for pleasant objects and we dislike unpleasant objects. Through the Buddhist teachings one learns that whatever arises is dependent on conditions. Sometimes there are conditions for the experience of pleasant objects and sometimes for the experience of unpleasant objects, nobody can exert control over the cittas which arise. Pleasant objects cannot last and therefore clinging to them will only lead to frustration and sadness. Time and again there is the arising of attachment, aversion and ignorance on account of objects experienced through eyes, ears, nose, tongue, body-sense and mind. There is enslavement to objects which arise and then fall away immediately. When the foolishness of such infatuation is realized, there are conditions to develop understanding of the realities of life. One will understand that there are countless akusala cittas arising on account of the objects experienced through the senses, akusala cittas which were not noticed before. When the characteristics of kusala and akusala are seen more clearly, there are conditions for the development of the roots of non-attachment, non-aversion and wisdom. These are the roots of kusala cittas which motivate the abstaining from unwholesome actions and the performing of wholesome deeds and speech.

As we have seen, there is a great variety of cittas. All cittas have in common that they cognize an object, but cittas are different as they are accompanied by different mental factors and experience different objects. Seeing always experiences visible object and hearing always experiences sound, but the reactions towards the objects and the thoughts about them vary for different people. When someone else, for example, speaks harsh words, there is the hearing of sound, and afterwards there is thinking of the meaning of the words, thinking of the person who speaks, thinking of conventional realities. Each person lives in his own world of thinking. We react to what is experienced not only with our thoughts, but also with action and speech. At the moments we do not perform good deeds or we do not develop understanding, we think, act and speak with akusala cittas. Citta determines our behaviour, citta is called in the scriptures "the leader of the world". We read in the *Kindred Sayings* (I, Sagāthā-vagga, Chapter I, The Devas, Part 7, §2, Citta), the following verse:

> Now what is that whereby the world is led?
> And what is that whereby it is drawn along?
> And what is that above all other things
> That brings everything beneath its sway?
>
> It is citta whereby the world is led,
> And by citta it is drawn along,
> And citta it is above all other things
> That brings everything beneath its sway.

In order to understand our own life and the lives of others, it is essential to understand what citta is. In order to have more understanding of what citta is, the difference between conventional truth and ultimate truth has to be known. Conventional truth is the truth we were always familiar with before we studied the Buddhist teachings; it is the conventional world of person, of "self", of things which exist. Ultimate truth are mental phenomena and physical phenomena. Cittas are mental phenomena, they experience something. Bodily phenomena, such as the sense organs, and physical phenomena outside do not experience anything. Citta can experience both mental phenomena and physical phenomena. The physical phenomena and mental phenomena of our life arise, exist just for an extremely short moment and then vanish. Ultimate realities have each their own characteristic which can be directly experienced when it appears, without the need to think about it. By theoretical understanding we will not know what citta is. Only if there can be the development of direct understanding of the citta appearing at this moment, no matter it is seeing, hearing or thinking, will we truly know what citta is. When the diversity of cittas and their manifold conditions are seen more clearly the truth of non-self will gradually be better understood. One will be motivated to seek the elimination of delusion about the realities of one's life, of the wrong view of self, of all forms of clinging, aversion and ignorance.

Chapter 5

Deeds and their Results

There are many types of cittas, moments of consciousness. Cittas can be kusala, wholesome, akusala, unwholesome, or neither kusala nor akusala. The sense impressions such as seeing or hearing are neither kusala nor akusala, but shortly after they have arisen and fallen away there are cittas which react to the object experienced by the sense impressions, and they react either in a wholesome way or in an unwholesome way. There are more often akusala cittas which can be rooted in attachment, aversion or ignorance, than kusala cittas which are rooted in non-attachment and non-aversion, and which may be rooted in wisdom as well. Akusala cittas can motivate evil deeds and kusala cittas can motivate good deeds. We read in the *Gradual Sayings* (V, Book of the Tens, Ch. 17, §8, Due to greed, hatred and delusion) that the Buddha said to the monks:

> Monks, the taking of life is threefold, I declare. It is motivated by greed, hatred and delusion. Taking what is not given...sexual misconduct...falsehood...harsh language...idle speech...covetousness...ill-will and wrong view is threefold, I declare. It is motivated by greed, hatred and delusion.
> Thus, monks, greed is the originator of a chain of causal action, hatred is the originator of a chain of causal action, delusion is the originator of a chain of causal action. By destroying greed, hatred and delusion comes the breaking up of the chain of causal action.

We read about a "chain of causal action". The Pāli term kamma also known in its Sanskrit form karma, literally means action or deed. A good deed brings a pleasant result and a bad deed brings an unpleasant result. The results of our own deeds come to us sooner or later, this is the law of kamma and result, and nobody can alter the operation of this law. The Buddha's teaching on kamma and result is difficult to grasp. It is not a dogma one has to accept. There can be theoretical understanding of kamma and result, but by theoretical understanding this law cannot be fully comprehended. Only by direct understanding of the physical phenomena and mental phenomena of our life the condition of kamma which produces result can be seen more clearly. Therefore it should not be expected that the law of kamma and result can be fully understood when we begin to investigate the Buddha's teaching on this subject.

A deed done in the past can produce result later on. Kamma can be compared to a seed developing into a tree which bears fruit later on. Evenso, a bad deed, for example killing, can produce an unpleasant result such as illness or pain. A good deed, for example a deed of generosity, can produce a pleasant result, such as the receiving of beautiful things. When we think of a deed and its result we usually think of a deed which has an effect on someone else. In order to understand the law of kamma and its result we should not think in terms of the conventional realities of persons and situations, but we should have understanding of the ultimate realities of cittas and their accompanying mental factors and of physical phenomena, realities which arise and then fall away immediately. We cannot be sure whether someone else performs kusala kamma or not from the outward appearance of things. We may see someone else giving things away but there may not be the performing of a deed of generosity. The giving may be motivated by selfish motives, and then giving is not kusala kamma. It is the wholesome or unwholesome intention or volition which constitutes kusala kamma or akusala kamma. The terms kusala kamma and akusala kamma can be used in the sense of good deeds and evil deeds, but when we are more precise kamma is the intention or volition motivating deeds performed through bodily action, through speech and through the mind. When we speak of the different types of kusala kamma and akusala kamma we should remember that kamma is intention or volition, a mental reality. Kamma is a mental factor accompanying citta, and it arises and falls away together with the citta.

How can a deed performed in the past produce its result later on? Kamma, or the volition which accompanies the citta when a good deed or a bad deed is performed, falls away immediately together with the citta. However, since each citta which falls away is succeeded by the next citta, kamma can be accumulated from moment to moment. Its dynamic force is carried on and when the time is ripe it can produce its result. That is the chain of causal action we read about in the above quoted sutta. The same sutta mentions the kinds of akusala kamma performed through body, speech and mind. Not every akusala citta is of the intensity of akusala kamma which can produce a result. When there is clinging to a pleasant sight or sound there is akusala citta but not akusala kamma which could produce a result. Clinging, however, has many degrees. It can be more subtle or it can be strong, such as covetousness, the desire for someone else's property. This has the intensity of akusala kamma when one plans to take away what belongs to someone else. Kusala kamma comprises abstaining from evil deeds as well as the performing of good deeds, deeds of generosity and mental development, such as the study of the Buddha's teachings and the development of understanding of the realities of our life.

Moments of happiness and misery alternate in our life. The experiences of pleasant objects and unpleasant objects through the senses do not occur by chance, they must have a cause: kamma is the cause. We read in the *Gradual Sayings* (IV, Book of the Eights, Chapter I, §5, Worldly Failings) that the Buddha said to the monks:

Monks, these eight worldly conditions obsess the world; the world revolves round these eight worldly conditions. What eight?
Gain and loss, fame and obscurity, blame and praise, bodily ease and pain.
Monks, these eight worldly conditions obsess the world, the world revolves round these eight worldly conditions.

Gain, loss, obscurity and fame,
And censure, praise, bodily ease, pain-
These are man's states—impermanent,
Of time and subject unto change.
And recognizing these the sage,
Alert, discerns these things of change;
Fair things his mind never agitate,
Nor foul his spirit vex. Gone are
Compliance and hostility,
Gone up in smoke and are no more.
The goal he knows. In measure full
He knows the stainless, griefless state.
Beyond becoming has he gone.

The person who has reached the state of perfection has equanimity towards the vicissitudes of life. He is freed from the chain of causal action, there is no more rebirth for him. So long as one is full of attachment, aversion and ignorance, one wants pleasant objects and dislikes unpleasant objects. However, the experience of pleasant objects and unpleasant objects is not in any one's power, it depends on kamma which produces result. One day there is gain, the next day loss; one day there is praise, the next day blame. Sometimes we are healthy, sometimes we suffer from sickness and pain. The experience of pleasant or unpleasant objects through the senses is not a reward or a punishment. The idea of reward or punishment stems from the conception of a supreme being, a God, who is the judge of man's deeds. The cause of the experience of pleasant and unpleasant objects through the senses is within ourselves: it is kamma. There is seeing and hearing of pleasant and unpleasant objects time and again. Seeing and hearing are the results of kusala kamma or akusala kamma. These results arise just for a moment and then they fall away. When we define what was seen or heard or think of the nature of the object, the moments of result have fallen away already. It is hard to tell whether seeing or hearing is the result of kusala kamma or of akusala kamma. Thinking of what was seen or heard is not result; when there is thinking there is kusala citta or akusala citta, but mostly akusala citta. In order to understand the ultimate realities of kamma and its result we have to be very precise. Seeing, hearing, smelling, tasting and the experience of tangible object through the body-sense are cittas which are results of kamma. Our reactions in a wholesome or in an unwholesome way to the objects which are experienced are not results of kamma, they are kusala citta or akusala citta. Kusala citta and akusala citta can be called the active side of life, since they can perform good deeds and bad deeds which will cause the appropriate results later on. The cittas which are results of one's deeds can be called the passive side of life. We have to receive results, whether we like it or not.

Cittas arise because of their own conditions, they are beyond control. Sometimes it seems that we ourselves can cause the enjoyment of pleasant objects. However, there have to be the right conditions for the enjoyment of pleasant objects and enjoyment cannot last as long as we wish. We can enjoy pleasant music by turning on the radio, but kamma is the cause of hearing, not a self. It also depends on conditions whether we can afford a radio or not. One may live in poverty and not be able to afford a radio. It is due to kamma if one is born into a poor family and has to live in uncomfortable circumstances. It is due to kamma if one is born into a family which is well-to-do and if one can live in comfort.

In order to understand that birth in pleasant surroundings and in unpleasant surroundings is the result of kamma we have to go back to the first moment of a lifespan. There was a citta at the first moment of our life, and this is the rebirth-consciousness. This citta must have a cause and the cause is in the past, it is kamma. Birth is result, we could not select our parents, nor time and place of our birth. The first moment of life is called rebirth-consciousness because there is not only this present life, there were also past lives. It is difficult to understand that kamma of the past produces the birth of a being. We can notice, however, that people are born in different circumstances, with different bodily features and different mental capacities. This does not happen by chance, there must be conditions for such differences. There are different kammas which cause different kinds of birth. In the "Discourse on the Lesser Analysis of Deeds" (Middle Length Sayings III, number 135) we read that Subha asks the Buddha what the cause is of the different results human beings experience from the time of their birth:

> "Now, good Gotama, what is the cause, what is the reason that lowness and excellence are to be seen among human beings while

Chapter 5 • Deeds and their Results

they are in human form? For, good Gotama, human beings of short lifespan are to be seen and those of long lifespan; those of many and those of few illnesses; those who are ugly, those who are beautiful; those who are of little account, those of great account; those who are poor, those who are wealthy; those who are of lowly families, those of high families; those who are weak in wisdom, those who are full of wisdom."

The Buddha answered Subha:

"Deeds are one's own, brahman youth, beings are heirs to deeds, deeds are matrix, deeds are kin, deeds are arbiters. Deed divides beings, that is to say by lowness and excellence."

Some people are born in countries where there is war and famine, others in countries where there is peace and prosperity. This does not happen by chance; kamma, a deed performed in the past, is the cause. If kamma is the cause of birth, what is then the role of the parents? Parents are also a condition for the birth of a child, but they are not the only condition. Kamma produces at the first moment of life the citta which is the rebirth-consciousness. The new human being which comes to life consists of mental phenomena and bodily phenomena. The physical phenomena which arise at the first moment of life must have a cause: kamma is the cause. Thus, at the first moment of life there is mental result as well as physical result of kamma. Kamma is not the only factor from which bodily phenomena originate. There are four factors in all: kamma, citta, temperature and nutrition. After kamma has produced bodily phenomena at the first moment of life, the other factors also produce bodily phenomena. As to the factor of temperature, there has to be the right temperature for the new being in the womb in order to develop. When the mother takes food, nutrition is suffused in the body and then nutrition is also producing bodily phenomena for the being in the womb. Citta is a condition as well for bodily phenomena arising throughout our life. If there were no citta we could not stay alive, we could not move, we could not perform any activities. If we remember the four factors which produce bodily phenomena, namely kamma, citta, temperature and nutrition, it will help us to understand the Buddha's teaching that the body does not belong to a self. What we call "my body" consists of bodily phenomena which arise because of different conditions and then fall away.

Kamma produces bodily phenomena at the first moment of a lifespan and also throughout life. It is kamma which produces the sense organs of eye-sense, ear-sense, smelling-sense, tasting-sense and body-sense. The sense organs which are the physical results of kamma are the means for the experiences which are the mental results of kamma: seeing, hearing and the other sense impressions. Thus, kamma produces result at the first moment of life, it produces the births of beings, and in the course of life it also produces pleasant and unpleasant results in the form of experiences through the senses.

Kamma can cause rebirth in unhappy and in happy planes of existence. Besides the human plane of existence there are other planes of existence. Birth in an unhappy plane is the result of akusala kamma and birth in a happy plane is the result of kusala kamma. Hell planes and the animal world, for example, are unhappy planes. The human plane and heavenly planes are happy planes. It may be felt by some that the existence of hell planes and heavenly planes is mythology. It should be remembered that conventional terms are used to designate different degrees of unpleasant results and pleasant results of kamma. Birth in a hell plane is an unhappy rebirth because in such a plane there are conditions for the

Chapter 5 • Deeds and their Results

experience of intense suffering. Birth in a heavenly plane is a happy rebirth because in such a plane there are conditions for the experience of pleasant objects. Life in a hell plane or in a heavenly plane does not last forever. There will be rebirth again and it depends on kamma in which plane rebirth-consciousness will arise. Birth in the human plane is the result of kusala kamma, but in the course of life there are conditions for the experience of both pleasant and unpleasant objects through the senses, depending on the different kammas which produce them.

It may happen that someone who has obtained wealth with dishonest means lives in luxury. How can bad deeds have pleasant results? It is not possible for us to find out which deed of the past produces its corresponding result at present. A criminal can receive pleasant results but these are caused by good deeds. His bad deeds will produce unpleasant results but it is not known when. In the course of many lives good deeds and bad deeds were performed and we do not know when it is the right time for a particular kamma to produce result. A good deed or a bad deed may not produce result during the life it was performed, but it may produce result in the following life or even after countless lives have passed. In the scriptures it is said that when kamma has ripened its fruit is experienced. We read in the *Dhammapada*, (verses 119 and 120):

Even an evil-doer sees good so long as evil ripens not; but when it bears fruit, then he sees the evil results.

Even a good person sees evil so long as good ripens not; but when it bears fruit, then the good one sees the good results.

Several other conditions are needed for akusala kamma or kusala kamma to produce their appropriate results. The time when one is born or the place where one is born can be a favourable or an unfavourable condition for kusala kamma or for akusala kamma to produce result. For example, when one lives in a time of war there are more conditions for akusala kamma and less conditions for kusala kamma to produce result. A particular kamma may be prevented from producing result when there is a very powerful counteractive kamma which has preponderance. For example, when someone is wealthy and lives in comfort, there are pleasant results for him, caused by kusala kamma. However, he may suddenly lose his wealth and be forced to live in miserable circumstances. His loss is caused by akusala kamma which has ripened so that it can produce unpleasant result. This is an example which shows that the way different kinds of kamma operate in our life is most intricate.

Time and again there is result in the form of the experience of pleasant and unpleasant objects through the senses and after such experiences there are kusala cittas or akusala cittas, but more often akusala cittas. There is likely to be attachment to pleasant objects and aversion towards unpleasant objects. Like and dislike alternate in our life. Attachment and aversion are of many degrees, they do not always have the intensity to motivate evil deeds. In that case there is no accumulation of kamma, but there is accumulation of defilements. Attachment and aversion arise and then fall away, but the conditions for these defilements are accumulated so that they can arise again. There are different types of condition which operate in our life. Kamma is one type of condition, it can produce result in the form of rebirth, or, in the course of life, in the form of the experience of pleasant or unpleasant objects through the senses. Defilement is another type of condition, it is the condition for the arising again of defilements. On account of pleasant and unpleasant results of kamma defilements may arise which are so strong that they motivate the committing of evil deeds. Thus, the result of kamma can condition defilements and defilements can condition the committing of akusala kamma which will in its turn produce result. This process is like an ever-turning wheel.

The Buddha's teaching on past lives, the present life and future lives, on the cycle of birth and death, is difficult to grasp. We can have more understanding of this teaching if we can see that, in the ultimate sense, life lasts merely as long as one moment of citta which arises and falls away. We are used to thinking in conventional terms of person, situation, life and death. In the conventional sense life starts at the moment of conception and it ends at the moment of death. In the ultimate sense there is birth and death at each moment a citta arises and falls away. The citta which has fallen away conditions the arising of the next citta. There has to be a citta arising at each moment, there is no moment without citta. Cittas arise in succession in the current of life. When the end of a lifespan approaches, the last citta, the dying-consciousness, falls away, but it is succeeded by the next citta. That citta is the first citta of a new life, namely the rebirth-consciousness. There can be theoretical understanding of death and rebirth, but all doubts can only be eliminated by the development of direct understanding of the mental phenomena and physical phenomena which arise and fall away. If there is direct understanding of the conditions for the citta which arises at this moment, doubt about rebirth can be eliminated. Just as the citta of this moment is succeeded by the next citta, evenso the last citta of this life will be succeeded by a following citta, the rebirth-consciousness.

It is dukkha to be in the cycle of birth and death. Why do we have to receive an unpleasant result of a deed committed in a past life? In a past life one was another being, different from what one is now. But why should we receive the result of a deed committed in the past by another being? A deed in the past which produces result now was committed by a being from which we have originated. It is indeed sorrowful that unpleasant results have to be received for evil deeds which may have been committed many lives ago. This is the law of kamma and its result, and it operates, whether we like it or not. A person in this life is different from what he was in a past life, but all that was accumulated in the past, kusala kamma and akusala kamma, defilements and good qualities, all accumulations have been carried on from moment to moment and they condition what is called the present personality. The *Path of Purification* (XVII, 167) explains:

> And with the stream of continuity there is neither identity nor otherness. For if there were absolute identity in a stream of continuity, there would be no forming of curd from milk. And if there were absolute otherness, the curd would not be derived from milk...So neither absolute identity nor absolute otherness should be assumed here.

The rebirth-consciousness has not been transferred from the past life to this life, it is completely new. However, the conditions for its arising stem from the past. The *Path of Purification* (166) illustrates this with similes. An echo is not the same as the sound but it originates from the sound. The impression of a seal stamped on wax is not the same as the seal itself, but it originates from the seal. These similes clarify that the present life is different from the past life, but that it is conditioned by the past. There is no transmigration or reincarnation of a self. The person who is reborn consists of five "groups of existence", the "khandhas", namely physical phenomena and mental phenomena which are arising and falling away. There is no permanent, unchanging substance which passes from one moment to the next one, from the last moment of life to the first moment of a new life. We read in the scriptures about the former lives of the Buddha and his disciples. The "Birth Stories" relate the former lives of the Buddha when he was still a Bodhisatta and accumulated wisdom and all the other excellent qualities, the "perfections", which were the right conditions to become a Buddha in his last life. There were accumulations of wisdom and of the perfections, but not a person, not a self who accumulated these. There were only the khandhas arising and falling away. Since each citta is succeeded by the next one within the current of countless lives, accumulations are carried on from one life to the next life.

Can one speak of evolution in the succession of different lives, a development from animal life to the human life and then to life in heavenly planes? There is no specific order in the kinds of rebirths, there is not necessarily development from life in lower planes to higher planes. In reality rebirth depends on the kamma which produces it. Kusala kamma may produce rebirth in a heavenly plane and after that it may be the right time for akusala kamma to produce rebirth in a hell plane. Only the person who has attained enlightenment has no more conditions for an unhappy rebirth. When one has reached the state of perfection all defilements have been eradicated and thus there are no more conditions for any kind of rebirth. This means the end of dukkha.

The Buddha, in the night he attained enlightenment, had penetrated the conditions for being in the cycle of birth and death and also the conditions for being freed from this cycle. Kamma which produces rebirth is part of a whole chain of conditions for the phenomena which constitute the cycle of birth and death. It is like a vicious circle of interdependently arising phenomena, forming a chain of twelve links, the first of which is ignorance and the last one death. This is called "Dependent Origination". The "Dependent Origination" is an essential part of the Buddha's teachings. Ignorance is mentioned as the first cause of the interdependently arising phenomena of the cycle. So long as ignorance has not been eradicated there are still conditions for the performing of kamma which produces rebirth. At rebirth there is the arising of mental phenomena and physical phenomena. There is the experience of objects through the senses and the mind-door. On account of the objects which are experienced different feelings arise and feeling in its turn conditions craving. Due to craving there is clinging which conditions the performing of kamma and this produces again rebirth. So long as there is birth there is old age and death, and thus there is no end to dukkha. This is the teaching on the "Dependent Origination" which shows the conditions stemming from the past life for phenomena in the present life, and conditions of the present life for phenomena in the future.

Ignorance is mentioned as the first factor of the Dependent Origination, but no first beginning of the cycle has been revealed. The *Path of Purification* (XIX, 20) explains:

> *There is no doer of a deed*
> *Or one who reaps the deed's result;*
> *Phenomena alone flow on—*
> *No other view than this is right.*

And so, while kamma and result
Thus causally maintain their round,
As seed and tree succeed in turn,
No first beginning can be shown.

It is of no use to speculate about the beginning of the cycle. The Buddha taught that when ignorance has been eradicated by wisdom, there aren't any more conditions for the performing of kamma, and thus no conditions for rebirth. Through wisdom there can be the reversal of the vicious circle made up by the links of the Dependent Origination. This means the end of the cycle, the end of dukkha. The commentary to the first book of the Abhidhamma, the *Expositor* (I, Part I, Chapter I, 44) explains by way of a simile the conditions leading to the continuation of the cycle and those leading to the end of it :

> ..."*leading to accumulation*" *are those states which go about severally arranging (births and deaths in) a round of destiny like a bricklayer who arranges bricks, layer by layer, in a wall.* "*Leading to dispersion*" *are those states which go about destroying that very round, like a man who continually removes the bricks as they are laid by the mason.*

When understanding has been developed to the degree that enlightenment is attained there will be "dispersion", the removal of the conditions for being in the cycle.

The teaching on the Dependent Origination explains why we are in this life, why we have to suffer old age, sickness and death. It explains the conditions for our life, for what we call our body and our mind. We may know in general that mind and body are dependent on conditions, but through the study of the Buddha's teachings we will know more in detail what these conditions are and how they operate from birth to death. It is kamma which produces bodily phenomena from the first moment of life and also throughout life. Besides kamma, citta, temperature and nutrition also produce bodily phenomena. Kamma produces throughout life the sense-organs, the physical conditions for the pleasant and unpleasant experiences which are the mental results of kamma. We are heirs to kamma, it is unavoidable that there are loss, pain and other adversities of life. There are many kinds of kamma which were performed in the past, and what is done cannot be undone. When it is the right time kamma produces its appropriate result. Ignorance of cause and result in life conditions aversion and frustration on account of unpleasant experiences and this means more suffering. Understanding of the cause of suffering does not mean the immediate elimination of grief and depression. However, understanding can help one to be less overcome by despair about what is unavoidable, what is beyond control. More understanding means less suffering. The Buddha did not only teach that life is dukkha, he also taught the release from dukkha, namely the development of the wisdom which can eradicate ignorance and all defilements.

Chapter 6

Good deeds and a wholesome life

> *Not to do evil, to cultivate good, to purify one's mind —*
> *this is the teaching of the Buddhas.*
>
> *(Dhammapada, verse 183)*

All religions encourage people to abstain from evil, to perform good deeds and to lead a wholesome life. In which way is Buddhism different from other teachings? What is kusala, wholesome, is kusala, and what is akusala, unwholesome, is akusala, no matter who performs it, no matter which religion he professes. Buddhism, however, is different from other teachings in so far as it explains the source of wholesomeness: the different cittas which perform good deeds. The Buddha explained in detail all the different cittas and their accompanying mental factors and also the conditions for their arising. He helped people to know the characteristic of kusala and of akusala. In that way the cittas which arise in daily life can be investigated and the different degrees of kusala and of akusala can be known by one's own experience. When we think of good deeds such as giving or helping, we usually have in mind the outward situation, we think of persons who perform deeds. The outward appearance of things, however, can be misleading. It depends on the intention or volition arising with the citta whether there is the performing of wholesomeness or not. Kusala kamma is an inward reality. We can only know ourselves the nature of our own citta. It is essential to know when the citta is kusala citta and when it is akusala citta.

The performing of what is wholesome comprises not only deeds of generosity but also good moral conduct as well as mental development. It is important to learn more details of the different ways of kusala which can be performed. In the Buddhist teachings the ways of wholesomeness can be classified as threefold, namely as **generosity, good moral conduct** and **mental development**. Learning about these ways is in itself a condition for the development of kusala in one's daily life.

The performing of deeds of **generosity** is included in the first of the threefold classification of wholesomeness, but the giving away of things may not always be kusala kamma. There may be moments of sincere generosity, but they are likely to be alternated with akusala cittas. We may expect something in return for our gift, and then there are akusala cittas rooted in attachment. Or we may find that our gift was too expensive and we may feel regret about it. Then there are akusala cittas with stinginess which are rooted in aversion. The person who receives our gift may not be grateful and therefore we may be annoyed or sad. We are inclined to pay attention mostly to the effect of our deeds on others. In order to develop what is wholesome there should be no preoccupation with the reactions of others towards our good deeds. Through the Buddhist teachings one learns to investigate the different moments of citta which motivate one's deeds. Generosity arises with kusala citta, it does not depend on gratefulness of other people. When one is intent on the development of what is wholesome, there will be no disturbance by other people's reactions. Is it not a selfish attitude to be constantly occupied with one's own cittas? On the contrary, when one comes to know when the citta is

Chapter 6 • Good deeds and Wholesome Life

kusala citta and when akusala citta, one will be able to develop more wholesomeness and this is beneficial for oneself as well as for one's fellowmen. We have accumulated countless defilements and thus the arising of kusala citta is very rare. When there are conditions for generosity, there are at such moments no stinginess, no clinging to one's possessions. The development of kusala promotes a harmonious society.

Generosity is an inward reality, it arises with kusala citta. Even when there is no opportunity for the giving of material things to others there are other ways of generosity which can be developed. The appreciation of someone else's good deeds which can be expressed by words of approval and praise is a way of generosity. I learnt of this way of kusala in Thailand where it is widely practised. People bow their head with clasped hands and say, "anumodana", which is the Pāli term for thanksgiving or satisfaction. In this way they express their appreciation of someone else's kusala. At such a moment the citta is pure, free from jealousy or stinginess. One may be stingy not only with regard to possessions, but also with regard to words of praise. Appreciation of someone else's kusala is one way of eliminating stinginess. When one learns of this way of kusala there will be more conditions for speaking about others in a wholesome way. We are inclined to speak about other people's akusala, but when we have confidence in the benefit of kusala we can change our habits. We can learn to speak in the wholesome way.

Another way of generosity is giving other people the opportunity to appreciate one's good deeds. Is this not a condition for pride? When one tries to impress others there is akusala citta. However, when one has the sincere inclination to help others to have kusala citta it is a way of generosity which is called "the extension of merit". It depends on the citta whether there is this way of kusala or not. Extension of merit does not mean that other people can receive the results of kusala kamma we performed. Each being receives the result of the kamma he performed himself. Extension of merit means helping others to have kusala citta on account of our kusala. In this way we can also help beings in other planes of existence, provided they are in planes where they can notice our good deeds and are able to appreciate them. In Buddhist countries it is a good custom to express with words and gestures the dedication of one's good deeds to the departed. When a meal or robes have been offered to monks, one pours water over one's hands while the monks recite words of blessing. In this way one expresses one's intention to dedicate one's kusala to other beings.

There are several more aspects of generosity. Abstaining from killing, lying and other evil deeds can be seen as an aspect of generosity. In abstaining from evil deeds which harm other beings one gives them a gift, one gives them the opportunity to live in peace. When we, for example, abstain from killing insects we give the gift of life. Another aspect of giving is forgiving the wrongdoings of someone else. When someone else speaks insulting words to us we may have aversion and conceit. When we think, "Why is he doing that to me", we think in terms of "he" and "me", and then there is comparing, which is conceit. Not only thinking of ourselves as higher than someone else, but also thinking of ourselves as equal or less than someone else, is conceit. Conceit prevents us from forgiving. When we are stubborn and proud, the citta is harsh, impliable. When we see the benefit of kusala we can forgive. At that moment the citta is gentle, without hate or conceit. One wishes the other person to be happy. For this way of generosity one does not have to look for material things to be given, it can be performed without delay. Knowing that forgiving is an act of generosity can inspire us to forgive more readily.

Another aspect of generosity, included in the first of the threefold classification of the ways of wholesomeness, is the explanation of Dhamma. When one explains the Buddha's teaching to others, one helps them to develop right understanding of the realities of life. This is the way leading to the elimination of suffering and therefore, the gift of Dhamma is the highest gift.

Not only generosity, but also **good moral conduct** is a way of wholesomeness. This is the second of the threefold classification of wholesomeness. There are many aspects to moral conduct or morality. Abstaining from evil deeds as well as good actions performed through body and speech are included in this way of kusala. We may believe that we are leading a wholesome life so long as we do not harm anybody. However, we should investigate whether the citta which arises is kusala citta or akusala citta. Then we will discover that we are full of defilements. The Buddha taught in detail on all unwholesome and wholesome mental factors which accompany cittas in different combinations. He explained all the different degrees of akusala and kusala. It is necessary to know whether kusala citta or akusala citta motivates our actions and speech, because the outward appearance of our actions and speech is misleading. We may speak in a pleasant way, but we may do so with selfish motives. We may flatter someone else in order to obtain a favour or in order to be liked by him. Then there is not wholesome speech, but speech motivated by attachment. We have to know our attachment, aversion, jealousy and conceit, we have to know all our defilements.

Abstaining from evil deeds is good moral conduct. There

are three unwholesome deeds performed through bodily action: killing, stealing and sexual misconduct. There are four unwholesome verbal actions: lying, slandering, rude speech and idle, useless talk. As regards killing, this is the killing on purpose of any living being, insects included. Also ordering someone else to kill is included in this type of akusala kamma. Does this mean that Buddhists should be vegetarians? The Buddha did not teach people to abstain from eating meat. The monks had to accept any kind of food which was offered to them by the layfollowers. The Buddha explained to the monks that they could eat meat unless they had seen, heard or suspected that an animal was killed especially for them. We read in the *Book of Discipline* (Vinaya IV, Mahā-vagga VI, on Medicines, 237) that the general Sīha attained enlightenment after having listened to the Buddha. He offered a meal which included meat to the Buddha and the order of monks. The Niganthas, who were of another teaching, found fault with the offering of meat. We read that after the meal the Buddha explained to the monks:

> "Monks, one should not knowingly make use of meat killed on purpose (for one). Whoever should make use of it, there is an offence of wrong-doing. I allow you, monks, fish and meat that are quite pure in three respects: if they are not seen, heard, suspected (to have been killed on purpose for a monk)."

This answer may not be satisfactory to everyone. One may wonder whether one indirectly promotes the slaughtering of animals by buying meat. It would be good if there were no slaughtering at all, no violence. The world, however, is not an Utopia. Animals are slaughtered and their meat is sold. If one in the given situation buys meat and eats it, one does not commit an act of violence. While one kills there is akusala citta rooted in aversion; killing is an act of

Chapter 6 • Good deeds and Wholesome Life

violence. While one eats meat there may be attachment or dislike of it, but there is no act of violence towards a living being.

The observing of precepts is included in good moral conduct. When one undertakes the observance of precepts one makes the resolution to train oneself in abstaining from akusala. There are precepts for monks, novices and nuns, and there are precepts for layfollowers. At the present time the order of nuns does not exist any more, although we can in Buddhist countries still see women who have retired from worldly life and try to live as a nun. The monks, as we will see, are under the obligation to observe many rules. For laypeople there are five precepts, but on special occasions they can undertake eight precepts. The precepts are not worded in the form of commandments, forbidding people to commit akusala. They are principles of training one can undertake with the aim to have less akusala.

The five moral precepts layfollowers can observe are the foundation for good moral conduct. When one undertakes them one makes the resolution to train oneself in abstaining from the following unwholesome deeds: killing living beings, stealing, sexual misconduct, lying and the taking of intoxicants, including alcoholic drinks. When one is in circumstances that one could commit an evil deed through body and speech but one abstains from it with kusala citta, there is good moral conduct.

Abstaining from slandering, rude speech and idle talk are not among the five precepts for laypeople. Abstaining from them, however, is kusala kamma. We may be in situations that we are tempted to speak evil, but when we abstain with kusala citta from slandering there is good moral conduct. When someone else scolds us we may abstain from talking back. However, if we keep silent with aversion there isn't good moral conduct. We have to investigate the citta in order to know whether there is good moral conduct or not. Abstaining from useless, idle talk is hard to observe. Most of the time we engage in idle talk about pleasant objects, such as delicious food, nice weather or journeys. We may think that such conversations are good since we do not harm other people. Through the Buddhist teachings we learn to investigate the cittas which motivate such conversations. We can find out that we speak mostly with attachment about pleasant objects and in this way accumulate ever more attachment. We do not have to avoid such conversations, but it is beneficial to know the nature of the citta which motivates our speech. When there are conditions for kusala citta we can speak about pleasant subjects with kindness and consideration for other people. Only the person who has reached the state of perfection has no more conditions to engage in idle talk. He has eradicated all kinds of akusala, also the subtle degrees.

Committing evil through bodily action or speech for the sake of one's livelihood is wrong livelihood. When one abstains from wrong livelihood there is right livelihood. One may, for example, be tempted to tell a lie in order to obtain more profit in one's business. If one abstains from such speech there is right livelihood.

It is hard to observe the precepts perfectly in all circumstances. If one has confidence in the benefit of kusala, one can gradually train oneself in observing the precepts. One may generally not be inclined to kill insects, but when one's house is full of fleas one may be tempted to kill. Killing may sometimes seem a quick and easy way to solve one's problems. One needs more effort to abstain from killing, but if one has confidence in kusala one will look for other ways to solve one's problems and abstain from killing. However, only those who have attained enlightenment will never transgress the five precepts, not even for the sake of their health or their life. The development of right understanding of the realities of our life leads to the perfection of moral conduct.

Paying respect to those who deserve respect is included in good moral conduct. In Buddhist countries it is a tradition to pay respect to parents, teachers, elderly people, monks and novices. At such moments there is an opportunity to give expression to one's appreciation for their good qualities, for their wisdom and guidance, and the assistance they have given. We see layfollowers paying respect to monks by clasping their hands and bowing their head, or by prostrating the body and touching the floor with the forehead, the forearms and knees. When one has not lived in a Buddhist country one may wonder why people are paying respect to monks in such a humble way. The monks have retired from worldly life in order to lead a life of detachment. Even if they are not perfect, they can remind us of those who have reached perfection. In Buddhist countries one can also see people prostrating themselves before a Buddha statue. This is not idol worship or a way of praying to the Buddha. One cannot pray to the Buddha since he is not in a heavenly plane or in any other place. He has passed away completely not to be reborn again. One can remember the Buddha's virtues, his wisdom, compassion and purity, and give expression to one's respect for his virtues in gesture and speech. It depends on the individual's inclination in which way he shows respect. One may show respect to someone out of selfish motives, such as desire for favours, but in that case the citta is akusala citta. When one pays respect or shows politeness with a sincere inclination, it is kusala citta. At such a moment there is no attachment or pride.

Another way of kusala kamma included in good moral conduct is helping other people through speech and deeds. In order to know whether there is this way of wholesomeness or not we have to investigate the cittas which motivate helping. One may help someone with selfish motives or with reluctance, and that is not kusala kamma. Helping with unselfish kindness is good moral conduct. At such a moment there is detachment. We are inclined to be lazy and to be attached to our own comfort, but in order to help someone we have to renounce our own comfort and make an effort for kusala. When kusala citta arises we are able to think of someone else's welfare. Also listening to other people when they talk about their problems and giving them our attention is a way of helping them.

In the Buddhist scriptures, including the *Jātakas* (the Buddha's Birth Stories), there are many practical guidelines for a life of goodwill and benevolence in one's social relations. There are guidelines for kings to reign with justice and compassion, and these can be applied by all in government service. We read in the "Kūtadanta Sutta" (Dialogues of the Buddha I, sutta 5) that the Buddha told the Brahman Kūtadanta about a King who wanted to offer a great sacrifice and asked his chaplain advice. The chaplain advised the King about a sacrifice for the sake of which no living being would be injured. He said to the King that, instead of punishing the bandits who were marauding the country, the King could improve the economic situation, a way which would be more effective in suppressing crime. The King should give grain to farmers, capital to traders, wages and food to those in government service. Then tensions would be solved and there would be an end to disorder. The King followed the chaplain's advice and made abundant gifts. The Buddha explained to Kūtadanta that a sacrifice is not only the giving of material things, but that it can also be dedication to spiritual matters, namely having confidence in the Buddha, the Dhamma and the Enlightened Ones, as well as mental development, including the development of the wisdom leading to perfection.

The "Sigālovāda sutta" (Dialogues of the Buddha III, number 31) contains the layman's social ethics. The Buddha explained to Sigāla that there should be love and goodwill in the relations between parents and children, teachers and pupils, husband and wife, employees and servants, laypeople and those who have retired from worldly life. The Buddha warned Sigāla of all the consequences of bad moral conduct and of the danger of evil friendship. A bad friend appropriates a friend's possessions, pays mere lip-service and flatters. Whereas a good friend gives good counsel, sympathizes and does not forsake one in misfortune, he is even willing to sacrifice his life for his friend. A good friend is intent on one's spiritual welfare. We read:

He restrains you from doing evil,
he encourages you to do good,
he informs you of what is unknown to you,
he points out to you the path to heaven.

The Buddhist principles of goodwill and tolerance can be applied in today's world in the community where one lives, on the national level and on the international level, including development cooperation. One can apply these principles more effectively if one at the same time develops understanding of the different cittas which arise, kusala cittas and akusala cittas. This understanding will prevent one from taking for kusala what is akusala. It is necessary to get to know the selfish motives with which we may act and speak, to get to know our many defilements. Otherwise our deeds and speech will not be sincere.

For a layman it is difficult to observe good moral conduct in all circumstances. He may find himself in situations where it is hard to abstain from akusala kamma, such as killing. The person who has inclinations to monkhood leaves the household life in order to be able to observe good moral conduct more perfectly. There is good moral conduct of the layman and there is good moral conduct of the monk. The monk's moral conduct is of a higher level. He leads a life of non-violence and contentment with little. He has renounced worldly life in order to dedicate himself completely to the study and practice of the Dhamma and to the teaching of it to layfollowers.

We read in the *Book of Analysis* (the Second Book of the Abhidhamma, 12, Analysis of Absorption) about the monk's life:

> *Herein a monk dwells restrained and controlled by the fundamental precepts, endowed with (proper) behaviour and a (suitable) alms resort, seeing danger in (his) slightest faults, guarded as to the doors of the sense faculties, in food knowing the right amount, in the first watch of the night and in the last watch of the night practising the practice of vigilance, with intense effort and penetration practising the practice of development of enlightenment states...*

The goal of monkhood is the eradication of all defilements through the development of wisdom, the attainment of the state of perfection. The monk is under the obligation to observe two-hundred and twenty-seven training rules. Apart from these there are many other rules which help him to reach his goal. They are contained in the Vinaya, the Book of Discipline for the monk. We read that every time a monk did not live up to the principles of monkhood, the Buddha laid down a rule in order to help him. The

Chapter 6 • Good deeds and Wholesome Life

Vinaya should not be separated from mental development, in particular the development of understanding of the mental phenomena and physical phenomena of life. Otherwise there would be the mere outward observance of the rules, no purification of the mind. How could one "see danger in the slightest faults" if there is no right understanding of the realities of his life, including the different cittas which arise?

The task of the monk is the development of understanding of the Dhamma and explaining the Dhamma to others. His task is the preservation of the Buddha's teachings. Social work is not the task of the monk, it is the task of the layman. The Rules of Discipline, dating from the Buddha's time about two-thousand five-hundred years ago, are still valid today. Shortly after the Buddha's passing away the first Great Council was held at Rājagaha under the leadership of the Buddha's disciple Mahā-Kassapa. We read in the *Illustrator of Ultimate Meaning* (commentary to the "Good Omen Discourse" of the "Minor Readings", of the *Khuddaka Nikāya*) that five hundred monks who had reached the state of perfection were to recite all the texts of the Buddha's teachings. We read that when Mahā-Kassapa asked which part they would rehearse first, the monks answered:

"The Vinaya is the very life of the Teaching; so long as the Vinaya endures, the Teaching endures, therefore let us rehearse the Vinaya first."

The monk should train himself in fewness of wishes. He is allowed the use of the four requisites of robes, almsfood, lodging and medicine, but they are not his personal property, they belong to the Order of monks. He is dependant on layfollowers for receiving these requisites and he should be contented with whatever he receives. These requisites are the monk's livelihood and he should train himself in purity of livelihood.

It is important also for laypeople to learn more about the monk's moral conduct. The monk and the layman have different lifestyles, but the layman can benefit from the study of the Vinaya and apply some of the rules in his own situation in daily life. The rules can also help the layman to "see danger in the slightest faults", to scrutinize his cittas when he, as a layman, is in similar situations as the monk. Both monks and laymen can train themselves in good moral conduct in action and speech as well as in wholesome thoughts. We read, for example, in the Vinaya (II, Suttavibhaṅga, Expiation XVI) that monks took possession of the best sleeping places, which were assigned to monks who were elders. The Buddha thereupon laid down a rule, stating that such conduct was an offence. Such an incident can also remind a layman not to ensure the best place for himself in a room, in a bus or train. One may think that one is entitled to the best place, but this is conceit. One can find out that there is at such a moment no kindness and compassion, but akusala citta. When we read in the Vinaya about the monk's daily life and about the situations where he was tempted to neglect his purity of moral conduct, we can be reminded of our own defilements, it can help us to recognize our deeply rooted faults and vices.

The monk should remember that the four requisites of robes, food, lodging and medicine are to be used so that he can stay healthy and dedicate himself to his task of the development of understanding of realities. The monk should not hint to lay-followers what kind of food he would like, he should not indulge in clinging to the requisites by hoarding food or robes. The monk should not try to obtain the requisites with improper means, such as by pretending to be more advanced in mental development than he really is. He may out of hypocrisy reject gifts, so that layfollowers believe that he is a person with fewness of wishes and then give to him more abundantly. The monk may try to impress others by his deportment. We read in the *Path of Purification* (I, 70):

> ...Here someone of evil wishes, a prey to wishes, eager to be admired, (thinking) "Thus people will admire me", composes his way of walking, composes his way of lying down; he walks studiedly, stands studiedly, sits studiedly, lies down studiedly; he walks as though concentrated, stands, sits, lies down as though concentrated...

The *Path of Purification* explains that desire for requisites can motivate speech with akusala citta. We read (I, 72) about different kinds of unwholesome speech:

> Ingratiating chatter is endearing chatter repeated again and again without regard to whether it is in conformity with truth and Dhamma. Flattery is speaking humbly, always maintaining an attitude of inferiority. Bean-soupery is resemblance to bean soup; for just as when beans are being cooked, only a few do not get cooked, the rest get cooked, so too the person in whose speech only a little is true, the rest being false, is called a "bean soup"; his state is bean-soupery.

Not only monks, also laypeople can be insincere in their deportment and speech in order to obtain something desirable. We should check whether our speech is "bean-soupery". We may to some extent speak what is true and to some extent what is not true. We may believe that there is no harm in "bean-soupery", but we accumulate at such a moment the tendency to lying.

The monk should train himself in virtue concerning the

requisites. He should use them without greed and reflect wisely on their use. We read in the *Path of Purification* (I, 85) about the use of almsfood:

> ...Reflecting wisely, he uses alms food neither for amusement nor for intoxication nor for smartening nor for embellishment, but only for the endurance and continuance of this body, for the ending of discomfort, and for assisting the life of purity...

Food is bound to be an object of attachment and it can also be an object of aversion. If one reflects wisely on the use of food there is kusala citta. It is natural that one enjoys delicious food, but if one remembers that food is like a medicine for the body, one will be less inclined to overeating, which is the cause of laziness. It is the monk's duty to reflect wisely on the use of the requisites, but also for laypeople there can be conditions for wise consideration of the things they use in daily life.

The monk should not indulge in sleep, in the company of people and in idle, useless talk. We read in the *Gradual Sayings* (V, Book of the Tens, Chapter VII, §9, Topics of talk) that while the Buddha was staying near Sāvatthī at Jeta Grove, some of the monks were indulging in idle talk, namely talk on kings, robbers, ministers, food, relatives, villages and other useless topics. The Buddha asked them what they were talking about and then said that such idle, useless talk was improper for them. He pointed out that there were ten topics of talk monks should engage in:

> Talk about wanting little, about contentment, seclusion, solitude, energetic striving, virtue, concentration, insight, release, release by knowing and seeing...

It is beneficial also for laypeople to find out which types of

Chapter 6 • Good deeds and Wholesome Life

citta motivate talking. Even though one cannot change one's habits yet, it is beneficial to know the different types of cittas which motivate one's actions and speech.

The monk should train himself in purity in all his actions and speech. There are four kinds of purification of the monk's moral conduct: restraint with regard to the disciplinary rules, the guarding of the sense doors, virtue concerning his livelihood, virtue concerning his requisites. With regard to the "guarding of the sense faculties", we read in the *Middle Length Sayings* (I, Sutta 27, The Lesser Discourse on the Simile of the Elephant's Footprint):

> ...Having seen visible object with the eye, having heard a sound with the ear, having smelt an odour with the nose, having tasted a flavour with the tongue, having touched a tangible object through the body-sense, having cognised a mental object through the mind, he neither adheres to the whole, nor to the details. And he strives to ward off that through which evil, unskilled states of mind, greed and sorrow, would predominate, if he remained with unguarded senses; and he watches over his senses, restrains his senses.

When there is understanding of visible object, sound and the other realities as they are, as impermanent and not self, one will be less infatuated by them. In this sense we have to understand the words "watching" and "restraint". It is by understanding, by wisdom, that there will be the "guarding of the sense faculties".

As we read in the *Dhammapada* (verse 183), it is the teaching of the Buddha to abstain from evil, to develop what is wholesome and to purify one's mind. Through **mental development** there can be purification of the mind, the elimination of what is impure, unwholesome. Mental development is the third of the threefold classification of the ways of wholesomeness. For mental development right understanding or wisdom is necessary, whereas the first way of wholesomeness, generosity, and the second way of wholesomeness, good moral conduct, can be performed also without right understanding. One may perform deeds of generosity, abstain from evil or help others because it is one's nature to do so, even without understanding of one's cittas. When there is right understanding of the different cittas which arise, there can be the development of more wholesome states. Through the development of understanding of one's cittas one will discover all one's weak points, even the slightest faults, and this means that there is less delusion about oneself. It is beneficial to discover that whenever there is no performing of kusala, our actions, speech and thoughts are akusala.

We read in the *Gradual Sayings* (Book of the Twos, Chapter 2, §7) about deeds of commission and omission. We read that the brāhmin Jānussoni asked the Buddha why some beings were reborn in Hell. The Buddha explained that it was owing to deeds of commission and omission. The Buddha said:

> *"Now in this connection, brāhmin, a certain one has committed bodily immoral acts, and omitted bodily moral acts...and the same as regards speech and thought. Thus, brāhmin, it is owing to commission and omission that beings...are reborn in Hell..."*

We read that the Buddha then explained that through the commission of kusala kamma and the omission of akusala kamma beings were reborn in Heaven. This text is a reminder not to neglect wholesome deeds. When there is omission of kusala, it will condition regret and worry later on. When kusala is performed with the aim to have less defilements, there will be more motivation to abstain from akusala, to develop kusala and to purify the mind. When more understanding of cittas and their accompanying mental factors is developed, confidence in the benefit of kusala will grow. When there is the direct realization of the truth of non-self, one will clearly see that kusala citta arises because of its own conditions, that there is no person or self who performs it. Then kusala will be purer, and moral conduct will become enduring. The understanding of the truth of non-self however, is the result of a gradual development, it cannot be realized within a short time. It is the development of direct understanding of the mental phenomena and physical phenomena of life. This is a way of kusala kamma which is included in mental development.

Selfishness, envy, stinginess, anger, conceit and other defilements disturb our social life. Such defilements motivate us to engage in wrong action and wrong speech. In this way we harm both ourselves and others. If we train ourselves to live according to the principles of loving-kindness, compassion, tolerance and gentleness, as taught by the Buddha, our social life will improve. At the moment of the performance of wholesomeness, the citta is pure, without defilements; there is no attachment, no aversion or hate, no ignorance. We read in the *Dhammapada* (verses 3-5):

"He abused me, he beat me, he defeated me, he robbed me", the hatred of those who harbour such thoughts is not appeased.

"He abused me, he beat me, he defeated me, he robbed me", the hatred of those who do not harbour such thoughts is appeased.

Hatreds never cease by hatred in this world; by love alone they cease. This is an ancient principle.

We cannot live up to such high principles unless there is the development of understanding which will eventually lead to the eradication of defilements. We can, however, begin to apply ourselves to the ways of wholesomeness we are able to perform at this moment. All kinds of wholesomeness which are included in the threefold classification of generosity, good moral conduct and mental development are to the welfare of ourselves as well as our fellow beings.

Chapter 7

Mental development and meditation

Mental development is the third of the threefold classification of wholesomeness. Mental development includes tranquil meditation as well as the development of insight wisdom. The first way of wholesomeness, generosity, and the second way of wholesomeness, good moral conduct, can be performed also without understanding of the cittas which arise, of kusala and akusala. For mental development, however, understanding is necessary. The understanding which arises in mental development is of different degrees, as we will see.

The study of the Buddha's teachings, the Dhamma, and the explaining of it to others are included in mental development. When one listens to the explanation of the Dhamma and reads the scriptures, one learns what is kusala and what is akusala, one learns about kamma and its their results and about the ways to develop wholesomeness. One learns that realities are impermanent, suffering, dukkha, and non-self, anattā. In order to develop understanding of the Dhamma, one should not only listen, one should also carefully consider what one hears and test its meaning. Explaining the Dhamma to others is included in mental development. Both speaker and listener can benefit, because they can be reminded of the need to verify the truth of the Dhamma in their own life. Understanding acquired through the study of the Dhamma is the foundation for **tranquil meditation** and **insight meditation** which are also included in mental development.

Tranquil meditation[7] and **insight meditation**[8] have each a different aim and a different way of development. For both kinds of meditation right understanding of the aim and the way of development is indispensable. In tranquil meditation one develops calm by concentrating on a meditation subject in order to be temporarily free from sense impressions and the attachment which is bound up with them. Insight meditation is the development of direct understanding of all realities occurring in daily life. The goal of insight meditation is the eradication of wrong view and all other defilements. Insight or insight wisdom is not theoretical understanding of mental phenomena and physical phenomena, it is understanding which directly experiences the characteristics of realities.

There are many misunderstandings with regard to the word "meditation". Some people want to meditate without understanding what meditation is, what its object and its aim are. Meditation is seen as escapism, a way to be free from the problems of daily life. One believes that when one sits in a quiet place and concentrates on one object one can become relaxed and free from worry. Relaxation is desirable, but it is not the aim of mental development.

As regards tranquil meditation, this is the development of calm. It is essential to have right understanding of what calm is. True calm has to be wholesome, it is freedom from defilements. As I explained before, akusala citta can be rooted in three unwholesome roots: attachment, aversion and ignorance. These roots have many degrees, they can be coarse or more subtle. Kusala citta is rooted in the wholesome roots of non-attachment and non-aversion and it may be rooted as well in wisdom or understanding. In order to have right understanding of one's cittas one

---
[7] In Pāli: samatha.
[8] In Pāli: vipassanā

Chapter 7 • Mental Development and Meditation 105

should investigate them in daily life. Otherwise one may take for kusala what is akusala. It is generally believed that if there is no aversion, no annoyance, there is calm. One should know, however, that when there is no aversion there is not necessarily kusala citta. There may be a subtle attachment to silence and then there is akusala citta, no calm. Calm is among the wholesome mental factors arising with each kusala citta. For example, when there is generosity and when there is good moral conduct, there is also calm. At such moments there are no attachment, aversion and ignorance, the citta is pure. The moments of kusala citta, however, are very rare, and soon after they have fallen away akusala cittas arise. Since the moments of calm arising with the kusala cittas are so few, the characteristic of calm may not be noticeable. The aim of tranquil meditation is to develop calm with a meditation subject. Only when there is right understanding of the difference between the moments of akusala citta and of kusala citta calm can be developed.

Even before the Buddha's time there were wise people who saw the disadvantages of sense impressions and the clinging to them. They were able to develop calm to a high degree, even to the degree of absorption[9]. Absorption is not what is generally understood as a trance. At the moments of absorption only the meditation subject is experienced and sense impressions such as seeing or hearing do not occur. The citta with absorption is of a plane of consciousness which is higher than the sensuous plane of consciousness, that is, the cittas of our daily life which experience sense objects. At the moments of absorption there is a high degree of calm, one is not infatuated with sense objects and defilements are temporarily subdued. There are different stages of absorption

---
[9] In Pāli: jhāna.

and at each subsequent stage there is a higher degree of calm. However, by absorption defilements cannot be eradicated. After the moments of absorption have fallen away, there are seeing, hearing and the other sense impressions again, and on account of them defilements arise again. Even if one has not accumulated the inclination and skill for the development of a high degree of calm, it is still useful to have some general knowledge about its development. This will help one to eliminate misunderstandings about tranquil meditation and insight meditation. It will help one to see the difference between these two kinds of meditation.

For tranquil meditation it is essential to have a keen understanding of the characteristic of calm and of the way to develop calm with a suitable meditation subject. The *Path of Purity* (Chapters IV-XII) describes forty meditation subjects which can condition calm. Among the meditation subjects are coloured disks (kasinas), recollection of the excellent qualities of the Buddha, the Dhamma and the enlightened disciples, meditations on corpses, mindfulness of death, loving-kindness, mindfulness of breathing. A meditation subject does not necessarily bring about calm. Only when there is right understanding of calm and the way to develop it, calm can grow. Moreover, it depends on a person's inclinations which meditation subject is suitable for him as a means to develop calm. It is generally believed that calm is developed by means of concentration. It should be known, however, that there can be right concentration and wrong concentration. Concentration is a mental factor which accompanies each citta. As I explained before, there is one citta arising at a time, but each citta is accompanied by several mental factors which each perform their own function while they assist the citta in experiencing an object. Each citta can experience only one object and it is concentration or one-pointedness which has the function of focusing on that object. Thus, concentration can be kusala, akusala or neither kusala nor akusala. When concentration accompanies akusala citta it is wrong concentration. If one tries very hard to concentrate there may be attachment to one's practice, or there may be aversion because of tiredness, and at such moments there is no calm. If there is right understanding of calm and of the way to develop it, there is also right concentration without there being the need to try to concentrate. It is right understanding which has to be emphasized, not concentration.

Mindfulness of breathing is generally believed to be an easy subject of meditation, but this is a misunderstanding; it is one of the most intricate subjects. If one tries to concentrate on breath without right understanding of this subject there will be clinging instead of calm. Breath is a bodily phenomenon which is conditioned by citta. It can appear as hardness, softness, heat or pressure. Those who want to develop this subject and have accumulated conditions to develop it have to be mindful of breath where it touches the tip of the nose or the upper-lip. However, breath is very subtle, it is most difficult to be mindful of it. The *Path of Purification* (VII, 208) states:

For while other meditation subjects become clearer at each higher stage, this one does not: in fact, as he goes on developing it, it becomes more subtle for him at each higher stage, and it even comes to the point at which it is no longer manifest.

We read further on (VIII, 211):

...But this mindfulness of breathing is difficult, difficult to develop, a field in which only the minds of Buddhas, "Silent

> Buddhas" [10], and Buddhas' sons are at home. It is no trivial matter, nor can it be cultivated by trivial persons. In proportion as continued attention is given to it, it becomes more peaceful and more subtle. So strong mindfulness and understanding are necessary here.

"Buddhas' sons" are the Buddha's disciples who had accumulated great wisdom and who were endowed with excellent qualities. Thus, this subject is not suitable for everybody.

We cling to breath since our life depends on it. Breathing stops when our life comes to an end. When this subject is developed in the right way, it has to be known when there is clinging to breath or to calm; it has to be known when there is akusala citta and when kusala citta. Otherwise it is impossible to develop calm with this subject. It is difficult to know the characteristic of breath, one may easily take for breath what is not breath. Following the movement of the abdomen is not mindfulness of breathing. Some people do breathing exercises for the sake of relaxation. While one concentrates on one's breathing, one cannot think of one's worries at the same time and then one feels more relaxed. This is not mindfulness of breathing, which has as its aim the temporary release from clinging. Mindfulness of breathing is too difficult for ordinary people and if one develops it in the wrong way, there is wrong concentration, there is no development of wholesomeness. For the development of this subject one has to lead a secluded life and many conditions have to be fulfilled.

Does one have to lead a secluded life for the development

---

[10] A Silent Buddha is an Enlightenment One who has found the Truth all by himself, but who has not accumulated excellent qualities to the extent that he can teach the Truth to others.

of all meditation subjects? There are different degrees of calm and if one has accumulated the inclination and capacity to cultivate a high degree of calm, even the degree of absorption, a secluded life is one of the conditions which are favourable for the attainment of it. However, only very few people can reach absorption, as the *Path of Purification* states. Even if one has no inclination to develop a high degree of calm there can be conditions for moments of calm in daily life. Some of the meditation subjects, such as the development of loving-kindness, can be a condition for calm in daily life. It is felt by some that for the development of this subject one has to be alone and one has to concentrate on thoughts of loving-kindness. The development of loving-kindness is not a matter of concentration but of right understanding. Loving-kindness can and should be developed when one is in the company of other people. It has to be clearly understood when there is unselfish kindness and when there is selfish affection. Moments of loving-kindness are likely to be followed by moments of attachment. Right understanding of one's different cittas is indispensable for the development of this subject, as it is for the development of all subjects of meditation. The *Path of Purification* (IX, 2) explains that in order to develop loving-kindness one should consider the danger of ill-will and the advantage of patience. It states that one cannot abandon unseen danger and attain unknown advantages. Thus we see again that right understanding is emphasized. We may dislike someone and we may be impatient about his behaviour. When we see the disadvantages of unwholesome thoughts there may be conditions for thoughts of kindness instead. That person may not treat us in a friendly way, but we can still consider him as a friend. True friendship does not depend on other people's behaviour, true friendship depends on the kusala citta. When we feel lonely, because we miss the company of friends, we should investigate our own citta. Is there loving-kindness with the citta? This point of view can change our outlook on our relationship with our fellowmen, and as a consequence our attitude can become less selfish. Loving-kindness can be extended to anybody, also to people whom we do not know, whom we pass on the street. We tend to be partial, we want to be kind only to people we like, but that is a selfish attitude. When there is true loving-kindness there is impartiality as well. We tend to think of others mostly with akusala citta, with cittas rooted in attachment or aversion. When we learn, however, what loving-kindness is, there can be conditions for wholesome thoughts instead, and then there is calm. Calm can naturally arise when there are the right conditions. When one tries very hard to have thoughts of loving-kindness in order to induce calm there is attachment instead of true calm which has to be wholesome. Thus, this is not the way to develop the meditation subject of loving-kindness.

Not all meditation subjects are suitable for everybody. There are meditation subjects on corpses in different stages of decay, but for some people such a subject can condition aversion instead of calm. Recollection on Death is a meditation subject which can condition calm in daily life. We are confronted with death time and again, and instead of sadness we can reflect with kusala citta on the impermanence of life. We can be reminded that even at this moment our body is subject to decay, constituted by physical phenomena, elements, which arise and then fall away. In the ultimate sense death is not different from what occurs at this moment.

Is it necessary to develop calm before one develops insight? Some people believe that when the mind is calm first, it will be easier to develop insight afterwards. It should be remembered that tranquil meditation and insight meditation have each a different aim and a different way of development. Tranquil meditation has as its aim to be free from seeing, hearing and the other sense impressions, in order to subdue clinging to sense objects. Insight meditation is the development of direct understanding of all realities of daily life: of seeing, hearing and the other sense impressions, of sense objects and also of the defilements arising on account of them. In this way the wrong view of self and all other defilements can be completely eradicated. Tranquil meditation should not be considered a necessary preparation for the development of insight. The Buddha did not set any rules with regard to tranquil meditation as a requirement for the development of insight. Individual inclinations are different. It depends on one's accumulated inclinations whether one applies oneself to tranquil meditation or not. People in the Buddha's time who had accumulated great skill developed calm even to the degree of absorption. In order to attain enlightenment, however, they still had to develop insight, direct understanding of realities, stage by stage. They had to have right understanding also of the citta which attained absorption in order not to take absorption for "self". There were many people in the Buddha's time who attained enlightenment without having developed a high degree of calm first.

The aim of tranquil meditation is the subduing of defilements, but, even when absorption is attained, they cannot be eradicated. When there are conditions, akusala cittas arise again. In the development of insight any reality which appears, no matter whether it is pleasant or unpleasant, kusala or akusala, is the object of understanding. Defilements should be understood as they are: as realities which arise because of their own conditions and which are not self. So long as defilements are still considered as "self" or "mine" they cannot be eradicated. The development of insight does not exclude calm, there are also conditions for calm in the development of insight. When defilements are eradicated stage by stage there will be more calm. When defilements are completely eradicated there is no more disturbance by akusala and this is the highest degree of calm.

The **development of insight** which is included in mental development, is the development of direct understanding of realities, of the mental phenomena and physical phenomena of our life. The development of calm could be undertaken also by people before the Buddha's time. Absorption was the highest degree of kusala which could be attained before the Buddha's enlightenment. The development of insight however, can only be taught by a Buddha. He taught the truth of impermanence, suffering, dukkha, and non-self, anattā. What is called a person or an ego is only a temporary combination of mental phenomena and physical phenomena[11] which arise and then fall away immediately. Through the development of insight there can be the direct experience of the truth and the eradication of defilements at the attainment of enlightenment.

When, however, understanding of realities is only theoretical, the truth of impermanence, dukkha and anattā is not grasped; there is still clinging to concepts and ideas of persons, the ego, the world. As I explained in chapter 3, there are two kinds of truths: the conventional truth and the ultimate truth. Conventional truth is the world of people and of the things around us, the world of houses, trees and cars, thus the things we have always

---

[11] Mental phenomena and physical phenomena are called in Pāli: nāma and rūpa.

been familiar with. When we study the Buddha's teachings we learn about ultimate truth. Ultimate realities are mental phenomena, cittas and their accompanying mental factors, and physical phenomena. Nibbāna is an ultimate reality but this can only be experienced when enlightenment is attained. Seeing is an ultimate reality, a citta which experiences visible object through the eye-sense. Seeing can only arise when there are eye-sense and visible object, it arises because of its own conditions. The same is true for hearing and the other sense impressions. There is only one citta at a time which experiences one object. After seeing, hearing and the other sense impressions there are kusala cittas and akusala cittas. Kusala cittas with generosity may arise, or akusala cittas with attachment, aversion or stinginess. All these realities arise because of their own conditions. There is no self who can control these realities or cause their arising. They arise just for a moment and then they fall away immediately. Because of ignorance we do not grasp the true nature of realities, their nature of impermanence, dukkha and non-self. Ignorance covers up the truth. Insight, the direct understanding of realities, is developed in order to eliminate ignorance and wrong view. Direct understanding of realities is different from theoretical understanding, but theoretical understanding is the foundation for direct understanding.

The object of insight, of direct understanding, is ultimate truth, not conventional truth. Conventional truth are concepts which are objects of thinking. For example, after seeing we think of the shape and form of a person or thing. That is not seeing, but thinking of concepts. The term concept stands for the idea which is the object of thinking as well as the name used to denote an idea. A concept is not real in the ultimate sense. Ultimate realities have each their own characteristic which is unchangeable, and which can be directly experienced when it appears. Seeing is an ultimate reality, it has its own characteristic. It is real for everybody. Its name may be changed, but its characteristic cannot be changed. Anger is an ultimate reality, it has its own characteristic which can be experienced by everybody. In order to be able to develop direct understanding of ultimate realities it is essential to know the difference between ultimate realities and concepts. One does not have to avoid thinking of concepts, because the thinking itself is an ultimate reality which arises because of its own conditions and which has its own characteristic. Thus, thinking can be the object of understanding when it appears. Every reality which arises because of conditions can be the object of direct understanding. Since concepts are not real in the ultimate sense and do not have characteristics which can be directly experienced, they are not objects of direct understanding.

How can direct understanding be developed? There has to be **mindfulness** or **awareness**[12] of the reality appearing at the present moment in order that direct understanding of it can be developed. There are many levels of mindfulness. It is a wholesome mental factor which accompanies each kusala citta. It is heedful or non-forgetful of what is wholesome. When there is mindfulness, the opportunity for wholesomeness is not wasted by negligence or laziness. Mindfulness prevents one from committing unwholesome deeds, it is like a "guard". There is mindfulness with generosity, with good moral conduct, and with the development of calm. In the development of calm there is mindfulness of the meditation subject, so that calm can develop. When insight, the direct understanding of realities, is developed, there is mindfulness

---

[12] In Pāli: sati

which is non-forgetful, aware, of the reality appearing at the present moment: a mental phenomenon or a physical phenomenon. At the very moment of mindfulness direct understanding of that reality can gradually develop. Thus, when there is mindfulness with the development of insight, the opportunity for the investigation of what appears at the present moment is not wasted.

Mindfulness and understanding are different realities, they are mental factors which each have a different function while they arise with kusala citta in the development of insight. Mindfulness is non-forgetful of the reality appearing at the present moment through one of the six doorways, but it does not have the function of understanding that reality. Understanding investigates the true nature of the reality which appears, but in the beginning it cannot be clear understanding. It is merely learning and studying the characteristic of the phenomenon appearing at the present moment. It develops very gradually, there are many degrees of understanding. The moment of mindfulness is so short, it falls away immediately. In the beginning mindfulness and understanding are still weak and thus one cannot be sure what mindfulness is.

Mindfulness in the development of insight is aware of one object at a time, either a mental phenomenon or a physical phenomenon. It is aware of an ultimate reality, not of a concept such as a person or a thing. The whole day there is touching of different things, such as a chair, a plate, a cup, a cushion. Usually there is thinking of concepts, one defines the things one touches, one knows what they are used for. When one has learnt about ultimate realities and there are conditions for mindfulness, however, it can be aware of one reality, such as hardness or softness appearing through the body-sense. At that very moment there can be a beginning of right understanding of that reality: it can be seen as only a physical reality, an element, arising because of conditions. One may touch a precious piece of chinaware, but it should be remembered that through touch the reality of hardness, not the chinaware, can be experienced. Hardness is tangible object, it is an ultimate reality which has its own characteristic. When there is mindfulness of that reality there is no attachment. When mindfulness has fallen away, there may be moments of thinking of that piece of chinaware, there may be thinking with attachment. Attachment to pleasant things is real, it does not have to be shunned as object of mindfulness. In order to develop understanding of ultimate realities it is essential to know when the object which is experienced is a concept and when an ultimate reality.

Mental phenomena and physical phenomena appear time and again. Through the body-sense hardness, softness, heat and cold can be experienced. They have their own characteristics and when mindfulness arises it can be directly aware of them. It can be verified by one's own experience that hardness is only a physical element, no matter whether it is in the body or in the things outside. Direct understanding of ultimate realities will gradually lead to detachment from the idea of "my body" and "my mind", from the idea of self. Through ear-sense sound is experienced. One usually pays attention to the origin or the quality of sound, one pays attention to the voice of someone or to music. At such moments there is thinking of concepts. When there are conditions for the arising of mindfulness, it can be aware of the characteristic of sound, a physical phenomenon which can be heard. It appears merely for a moment and then it falls away. Sound does not belong to anyone, it is merely an element, non-self. Is it helpful to know this? Knowing that even the sound of music one enjoys is only a physical

Chapter 7 • Mental Development and Meditation 117

element seems very prosaic. One can enjoy the pleasant things of life, but in between there can be a moment of developing understanding of ultimate realities. Sound is real, hearing is real, enjoyment of music is real, they are all realities which can be known as they are: impermanent and non-self. Different objects can be experienced through one doorway at a time. Hearing experiences sound through the ears. Seeing experiences visible object or colour through the eyes. Hearing cannot see, seeing cannot hear, there is only one citta at a time. There is no self who sees or hears, the seeing sees, the hearing hears. Through the development of insight one can verify that there is no self who coordinates seeing, hearing and all the other experiences. In the ultimate sense life is one moment of experiencing an object. When we are thinking of a person or a thing, we have an image of a "whole", and then the object at that moment is a concept. At the moment of mindfulness, however, only one reality at a time, appearing through one of the six doorways, is the object.

A mental phenomenon knows or experiences something, whereas a physical phenomenon does not experience anything. It is essential to learn the difference between these two kinds of phenomena. We tend to consider body and mind as a "whole", as a person or self. When there is mindfulness of one reality at a time, we learn that there are only different mental elements and physical elements arising and falling away. When sound appears there is also hearing, the experience of sound. Sound and hearing have different characteristics. Sound does not experience anything, whereas hearing experiences an object, the object of sound. When visible object appears there is also seeing, the experience of visible object. Visible object does not experience anything, whereas seeing experiences an object, visible object. When there is mindfulness it is aware of only one object, either a physical reality or a mental reality. Each citta experiences only one object, and thus when mindfulness accompanies the citta, it can be aware of only one object at a time. It is very difficult to distinguish sound from hearing and visible object from seeing. Only when insight, direct understanding of realities, has been developed, physical realities and mental realities can be distinguished from each other. So long as there is confusion about the difference between what is mental and what is physical, there is still an image or a concept of a "whole". When there is no precise understanding of one reality at a time, its arising and falling away, its impermanence, cannot be directly understood.

There is no self who can choose the object of awareness or who can direct mindfulness to such or such object. Mindfulness is non-self, it arises because of its own conditions. It is unpredictable of what object mindfulness will be aware: either a mental reality or a physical reality. The characteristic of mindfulness cannot be understood by theoretical knowledge, by describing its nature. Only when mindfulness arises can one know what it is. It arises when there are the right conditions. The right conditions are: listening to the Dhamma as it is explained by someone with right understanding, and studying and considering Dhamma. Theoretical understanding of ultimate realities and remembrance of what one has learnt are a necessary foundation for the development of direct understanding. If one has expectations about the arising of mindfulness, if one tries to concentrate on realities, or tries to observe them, there is clinging to an idea of self who can direct mindfulness, and this is counteracting to the arising of mindfulness.

Chapter 7 • Mental Development and Meditation

In the beginning one is bound to take for mindfulness what is not mindfulness but thinking. When one thinks, "This is attachment", there is no direct awareness of the **characteristic** of the reality which appears. There can still be a concept of "my attachment". Then attachment is not understood as a conditioned reality which is non-self. When one reality appears through one of the six doors, there can be a moment of investigation or study of its **characteristic**, and that is the beginning of understanding of its true nature, its nature of non-self. At such a moment there is mindfulness, mindfulness of the reality appearing at the present moment. Even one extremely short moment of mindfulness and investigation of an ultimate reality is beneficial, because in that way mindfulness and understanding can be accumulated. Then there are conditions for their arising again later and in that way direct understanding can grow.

Direct understanding of realities can develop only very gradually. There are different stages of insight, and in order that these stages can arise, understanding has to become very keen. The first stage of insight is the stage that the difference between the reality which is mental and the reality which is physical can be clearly distinguished. As I explained, this is difficult, since one tends to confuse realities such as seeing and visible object or hearing and sound. The arising and falling away, the impermanence of realities, can be penetrated only at a later stage of insight.

All the realities of one's daily life, also defilements, can be the objects of direct understanding. Defilements can eventually be eradicated when they are are understood as they are: as non-self. If one tries to change one's life in order to create conditions for insight, or if one tries to suppress defilements in order to have more awareness, one is led by clinging and this is not the right way. One should come to understand all realities, the mental and physical phenomena which naturally arise in daily life.

The development of insight, of direct understanding of realities, is very intricate and there cannot be an immediate result when one begins to develop it. Is it worth while to begin with its development, even though it takes more than one life to reach the goal? It is beneficial to begin with its development. Theoretical understanding does not eliminate delusion when there is seeing, hearing and the other experiences through the senses and the mind-door. On account of the objects which are experienced there is bound to be attachment, aversion and ignorance. If there is at least a beginning of the development of direct understanding we will be able to verify that our life is one moment of experiencing an object through one of the six doors. When there is seeing, its characteristic can be investigated. It can be understood that it is only a mental reality arising because of its own conditions, not a person or self. It sees what appears through eye-sense. When visible object appears it can be understood that it is only a physical reality, appearing through eye-sense, not a person or thing. All realities appearing through the six doors can be understood as they are, as non-self. Through direct understanding of realities wrong view about them can be eliminated.

We read in the *Kindred Sayings* (IV, Kindred Sayings on Sense, Third Fifty, Chapter 5, §152, Is there a Method?), that the Buddha spoke to the monks about the method to realize through direct experience the end of dukkha:

> "Herein, monks, a monk, seeing visible object with the eye, either recognizes within him the existence of lust, malice and illusion, thus: 'I have lust, malice and illusion,' or recognizes the non-existence of these qualities within him, thus: 'I have not lust, malice and illusion.'

Chapter 7 • Mental Development and Meditation

Now as to that recognition of their existence or non-existence within him, are these conditions, I ask, to be understood by belief, or inclination, or hearsay, or argument as to method, or reflection on reasons, or delight in speculation?"
"Surely not, lord."
"Are not these states to be understood by seeing them with the eye of wisdom?"
"Surely, lord."
"Then, monks, this is the method by following which, apart from belief... a monk could affirm insight thus: 'Ended is birth, lived is the righteous life, done is the task, for life in these conditions there is no hereafter.'"

We then read that the same is said with regard to the experiences through the doorways of the ears, nose, tongue, body-sense and mind. The development of understanding of all that is real, also of one's defilements, is the way leading to the eradication of defilements, to the end of rebirth. This is the end of dukkha.

Chapter 8

The eightfold Path

The development of the eightfold Path leads to the goal of the Buddha's teachings: the end of dukkha, suffering. As I explained in chapter 2, the Buddha taught the four noble Truths: the Truth of dukkha, of the cause of dukkha, which is craving, of the ceasing of dukkha, which is nibbāna, and of the Path leading to the ceasing of dukkha. We read in the *Kindred Sayings* (V, The Great Chapter, Kindred Sayings about the Truths, chapter II, §1) that the Buddha, while he was dwelling at Isipatana, in the Deerpark, spoke to the company of five monks:

Monks, these two extremes should not be followed by one who has gone forth as a wanderer. What two?

Devotion to pleasures of sense, a low practice of villagers, a practice unworthy, unprofitable, the way of the world (on the one hand); and (on the other) devotion to self-mortification, which is painful, unworthy and unprofitable.

By avoiding these two extremes the Tathāgata has gained knowledge of that middle path which gives vision, which gives knowledge, which causes calm, special knowledge, enlightenment, Nibbāna.

And what, monks, is that middle path which gives vision...Nibbāna?

Verily, it is this noble eightfold way, namely: Right view[13], right thinking, right speech, right action, right livelihood, right effort, right mindfulness, right concentration....

When there is direct awareness and right understanding of any reality which appears in daily life, there is at that

---
[13] Right understanding of realities.

moment no devotion to sense pleasures nor self-mortification. One is on the middle way, and that is the eightfold Path. When direct understanding of realities has been developed stage by stage, the wrong view of self can be eradicated. Then it is clearly understood that what is taken as a person or self are in reality merely mental phenomena and physical phenomena which arise and then fall away immediately. When the realities which arise because of their own conditions have been understood as they are, as impermanent, dukkha and non-self, there can be enlightenment, that is, the experience of nibbāna. Nibbāna is the unconditioned reality, the reality which does not arise and fall away. There are four stages of enlightenment and at these stages defilements are subsequently eradicated. First the wrong view of self has to be eradicated because the other defilements cannot be eradicated so long as they are taken for "self". All defilements are eradicated when the fourth and last stage of enlightenment has been attained, the stage of the perfected one, the "arahat". He has eradicated ignorance and all forms of clinging completely, there are no more latent tendencies of defilements left. Ignorance and clinging are conditions for rebirth again and again, for being in the cycle of birth and death. When ignorance and clinging have been eradicated there will be the end of the cycle of birth and death, the end of dukkha.

The development of the eightfold Path leads to the cessation of dukkha. In order to know what the eightfold Path is, the eight Path factors as enumerated in the above-quoted sutta have to be examined more closely. They are mental factors[14] which can accompany citta. As I explained before, there is one citta arising at a time, but it is accompanied by several mental factors which each

---

[14] In Pāli: cetasika.

perform their own function while they assist the citta in cognizing an object. Mental factors can be akusala, kusala or neither kusala nor akusala, in accordance with the citta they accompany. When the eightfold Path is being developed, the mental factors which are the Path factors perform their own specific functions in order that the goal can be attained: the eradication of defilements. From the beginning it should be remembered that there is no self, no person, who develops the Path, but that it is citta and the accompanying mental factors which develop it. As we read in the sutta, the eight Path factors are the following:

right understanding
right thinking
right speech
right action
right livelihood
right effort
right mindfulness
right concentration

Right understanding is the first and foremost factor of the eightfold Path. What is right understanding of the eightfold Path? There are many levels and degrees of understanding. There can be theoretical understanding of the Buddha's teachings on mental phenomena and physical phenomena. However, the Path factor right understanding is not theoretical understanding of realities. When it is developed it is the direct understanding of the true nature of physical phenomena and mental phenomena appearing in daily life. When right understanding begins to develop, however, it cannot yet be clear, direct understanding immediately. The mental phenomena and physical phenomena which appear in daily life have to be investigated over and over again. As I explained in chapter 7, not concepts but ultimate realities are the objects of direct understanding. The characteristics of seeing, visible object, hearing, sound, attachment or generosity can be investigated by right understanding of the eightfold Path. In that way they can be seen as only conditioned realities which are non-self. When there are conditions for the arising of right understanding it arises and investigates the reality which presents itself at that moment through one of the six doors. Right understanding arises and then falls away immediately together with the citta it accompanies, but it is accumulated and therefore there are conditions for its arising again. In this way understanding can develop; It develops, there is no person who develops it. Right understanding can penetrate the characteristics of impermanence, dukkha and non-self and it can eventually realize the four noble Truths.

Right thinking is another Path factor. Right thinking is not the same as what we mean by thinking in conventional sense. When we use the word thinking in conventional language we mean thinking of a concept, an event or a story. In the ultimate sense thinking is a mental factor which accompanies many types of citta, although not every type. Thinking "touches" or "hits" the object which citta experiences and in this way assists the citta in cognizing that object. The mental factor thinking experiences the same object as the citta it accompanies. The object can be a concept and also an ultimate reality, a mental phenomenon or a physical phenomenon. Thinking arises merely for an extremely short moment together with the citta and then it falls away with the citta. Thinking can be akusala, kusala or neither akusala nor kusala. When it is akusala it is wrong thinking and when it is kusala it is right thinking. The Path factor right thinking arises together with the Path factor right understanding. The object of the Path factor right thinking is an ultimate reality, the reality which appears at the present moment. In the beginning there will be doubt whether the reality appearing at the present moment is a physical reality, such as visible object, or a mental reality, such as seeing. When right understanding is only beginning to develop there is not yet precise understanding of the difference between the characteristics of these realities. The function of the Path factor right thinking is "touching" the reality appearing at the present moment so that right understanding can investigate its characteristic. In that way precise understanding of that object can be developed, until there is no more confusion between the characteristic of a mental reality and a physical reality. Right thinking assists right understanding to penetrate the true nature of realities: the nature of impermanence, dukkha and non-self. Thus we see that the Path factor of right thinking is essential for the development of understanding.

There are three Path factors which are the factors of good moral conduct[15]: right speech, right action and right livelihood. They have the function of abstaining from wrong speech, wrong action and wrong livelihood. Wrong livelihood is wrong speech and wrong action committed for the sake of one's livelihood. When there are conditions for abstaining from these kinds of akusala kamma the factors of good moral conduct perform the function of abstention. They arise one at a time. When there is abstention from wrong action such as killing, there cannot be at the same time abstention from wrong speech. The development of right understanding will condition good moral conduct, but only after enlightenment has been attained good moral conduct becomes enduring. The person who has attained

---
[15] In Pāli: sīla

the first stage of enlightenment has no more conditions for the committing of akusala kamma which can produce an unhappy rebirth. Thus, right understanding of realities bears directly on one's moral conduct in daily life. As we have seen, the three mental factors which are the abstentions from evil moral conduct arise one at a time, depending on the given situation. At the moment of enlightenment, however, all three Path factors which are good moral conduct arise together. The reason is that they perform at that moment the function of eradicating the cause of misconduct as to speech, action and livelihood. Latent tendencies of defilements are eradicated so that they do not arise anymore. As I explained before, defilements are eradicated at different stages of enlightenment and it is only at the fourth and final stage that all akusala is eradicated.

Right effort is another Path factor. Effort or energy is a mental factor which can arise with kusala citta, akusala citta and citta which is neither kusala nor akusala. Its function is to support and strengthen the citta. When effort or energy is kusala it is the condition for courage and perseverance in the performing of kusala. Energy is right effort of the eightfold Path when it accompanies right understanding of the eightfold Path. It is the condition for perseverance with the investigation and study of the reality appearing at the present moment, be it a mental phenomenon or a physical phenomenon. Energy and patience are indispensable for the development of right understanding. There must be awareness of mental phenomena and physical phenomena over and over again, in the course of many lives, so that right understanding can see realities as they are, as impermanent, dukkha and non-self. When we hear the word effort we may have a concept of self who exerts an effort to develop right

Chapter 8 • The eightfold Path 129

understanding. Effort is non-self, it is a mental factor which assists right understanding. When there is mindfulness of a reality and understanding investigates its nature, there is at that moment also right effort which performs its function. It does not arise because of one's wish, it arises because of its own conditions.

Right mindfulness is another factor of the eightfold Path. As I explained in chapter seven, there are many levels of mindfulness. There is mindfulness with each kusala citta and its function is to be heedful, non-forgetful of what is wholesome. Mindfulness is a factor of the eightfold Path when it accompanies right understanding of the eightfold Path. There may be theoretical understanding of realities acquired through reading and thinking. One may think in the right way of the phenomena of life which are impermanent and non-self. However, in order to directly experience the truth there must be mindfulness of the reality which appears at the present moment. The moment of mindfulness is extremely short, it falls away immediately. However, during that moment understanding can investigate the characteristic of the reality which appears, and in this way understanding can develop very gradually. Right understanding arises together with right mindfulness, but they have each a different function. Right mindfulness is heedful, attentive or conscious of the reality which appears but it does not investigate its nature. It is the function of right understanding to investigate and penetrate the true nature of the reality which appears at the present moment.

Right concentration is another factor of the eightfold Path. Concentration or one-pointedness is a mental factor arising with each citta. Citta experiences only one object at a time and concentration has the function to focus on that one object which citta experiences. Concentration can accompany kusala citta, akusala citta and citta which is neither kusala nor akusala. Right concentration is concentration which is wholesome. There are many kinds and degrees of right concentration. As we have seen in chapter 7, there is right concentration in tranquil meditation. When calm is developed to the extent that absorption is attained, there is a high degree of concentration which focuses on the meditation subject. There are no more sense impressions such as seeing or hearing and defilements are temporarily subdued. There is also right concentration in the development of direct understanding of realities. The Path factor right concentration accompanies right understanding of the eightfold Path. It focuses rightly on the reality which appears at the present moment and which is the object of right understanding. There is no need to make a special effort to concentrate on mental phenomena and physical phenomena. If one tries to concentrate there is clinging to an idea of "my concentration", and then there is no development of right understanding. When there are conditions for the arising of right mindfulness and right understanding, there is right concentration already which focuses on the reality presenting itself at that moment.

Some people believe that one should first develop morality, after that concentration and then right understanding. However, all kinds of kusala, be it generosity, good moral conduct or calm can develop together with right understanding. There is no particular order in the development of wholesomeness. Kusala citta is non-self, anattā. When one reads the scriptures one will come across texts on the development of right concentration which has reached the stage of absorption. This does not imply that all people should develop calm to the degree of absorption. As I explained in chapter 7, it depends on the individual's accumulations whether he can develop it or

Chapter 8 • The eightfold Path   131

not. The Buddha encouraged those who could develop calm to the degree of absorption to be mindful of realities in order to see also absorption as non self. There are many aspects to each subject which is explained in the teachings and one has to take these into account when one reads the scriptures. Otherwise one will read the texts with wrong understanding. The Buddha's teachings are subtle and deep, not easy to grasp. We read in the *Kindred Sayings* (V, The Great Chapter, Kindred Sayings about the Truths, chapter II, §. 9, Illustration) that the Buddha said to the monks:

Monks, the noble Truth of This is dukkha...This is the arising of dukkha...This is the practice that leads to the ceasing of dukkha, has been pointed out by me. Therein are numberless shades and variations of meaning. Numberless are the ways of illustrating this noble truth of, This is the practice that leads to the ceasing of dukkha. Wherefore, monks an effort must be made to realize: This is dukkha, This is the arising of dukkha, This is the ceasing of dukkha, This is the practice leading to the ceasing of dukkha.

The eightfold Path must be developed in daily life. One should come to know all realities, also one's defilements, as they arise because of their own conditions. One cannot change the reality which arises, it is non-self. Misunderstandings as to the development of right understanding are bound to arise if one has not correctly understood what the objects of mindfulness and right understanding are. Therefore I wish to stress a few points concerning these objects. Some people believe that a quiet place is more favourable for the development of right understanding. They should examine themselves in order to find out which types of citta motivate their thinking. If laypeople want to live as a monk in order to have more opportunity to develop right understanding, they are led by desire. It is due to conditions, to one's accumulated inclinations, whether one is a monk or a layman. Both monk and layman can develop understanding, each in his own situation. Then one will come to understand one's own accumulated inclinations. The development of the eightfold Path is the development of right understanding of all realities which arise because of their own conditions, also of one's attachment, aversion and other defilements. In order to remind people of the realities which can be objects of mindfulness and right understanding, the Buddha taught the "Four Applications of Mindfulness". These Four Applications contain all mental phenomena and physical phenomena of daily life which can be objects of mindfulness and right understanding. They are: Contemplation of the Body, which comprises all physical phenomena, Contemplation of Feeling, Contemplation of Citta and Contemplation of Dhammas, which comprises all realities not included in the other three Applications of Mindfulness. Contemplation in this context does not mean thinking of realities. It is direct awareness associated with right understanding. We read in the "Satipaṭṭhāna Sutta" (Middle Length Sayings I, 10) that the Buddha, while he was dwelling at Kammāsadamma, said to the monks:

> This is the only way, monks, for the purification of beings, for the overcoming of sorrow and lamentation, for the destruction of suffering and grief, for reaching the right path, for the attainment of nibbāna, namely, the Four Applications of Mindfulness.

The teaching on the factors of the eightfold Path as well as the teaching on the Four Applications of Mindfulness pertain to the development of right understanding of realities in daily life, but they each show different aspects.

The teaching on the Path factors shows us that for the development of right understanding there are, apart from the factor right understanding, other Path factors which are the conditions for right understanding to perform its function in order that the goal can be reached, the eradication of defilements. In explaining the Four Applications of Mindfulness the Buddha encouraged people to be mindful in any situation of their daily life. In the Contemplation of Citta is first mentioned citta with attachment and this can remind us not to shun akusala as object of mindfulness. The Buddha explained that there can be mindfulness of realities no matter whether one is walking, standing, sitting or lying down, no matter what one is doing. Those who develop tranquil meditation and attain calm, even to the degree of absorption, can be mindful of realities. The Buddha showed that there isn't any reality which cannot be object of mindfulness and right understanding. When one develops right understanding of any reality which appears there is no need to think of the Four Applications of Mindfulness or of the Path factors.

The Buddha's teaching on the development of right understanding of realities is deep, it is not easy to grasp what mindfulness and right understanding are. For this reason I would like to give a further explanation of objects of mindfulness which present themselves in daily life. Some people believe that mindfulness is being conscious of what one is doing. If one is conscious of what one is doing, such as reading or walking, there is thinking of concepts, no awareness of realities. There is clinging to an idea of self who reads or walks. No matter what one is doing there are mental phenomena and physical phenomena and understanding of them can be developed. When one, for example, is watching T.V., there can be thinking of a story which is being enacted. However, there is not only thinking, there are also seeing, visible object, hearing, sound, feeling or remembrance. Most of the time there is forgetfulness of realities, there is thinking of concepts. However, in between the moments of thinking there can be mindfulness of one reality appearing through one of the six doors, an ultimate reality which is either a mental reality or a physical reality. The characteristics of different realities can gradually be learnt. When we read a book we think of the meaning of the letters and of the story. But there are also moments of seeing merely what is visible, of what appears through eye-sense. It is because of remembrance that we know the meaning of what we read. Remembrance is a mental factor arising together with the citta, it is not self. Also remembrance can be understood as it is. It seems that thinking occurs at the same time as seeing, but they are different cittas with different characteristics.The characteristics of different realities can be investigated, no matter whether we are seeing, reading, hearing or paying attention to the meaning of words. When this has been understood we will see that objects of awareness are never lacking in our daily life. There are six doorways, there are objects experienced through these six doorways and there are the realities which experience these objects. That is our life.

Right understanding develops very gradually, it has to be developed during countless lives before it can become full understanding of all realities which appear. There are several stages of insight in the course of the development of right understanding. Even the first stage of insight, which is merely a beginning stage of insight, is difficult to reach. At this stage the different characteristics of the mental reality and of the physical reality which appear are clearly distinguished from each other. At each higher stage

Chapter 8 • The eightfold Path   135

of insight understanding becomes keener. The objects of understanding are the same: the mental phenomena and physical phenomena which appear, but understanding of them becomes clearer. When conditioned realities have been clearly understood as impermanent, dukkha and non-self, there can be the experience of nibbāna, the unconditioned reality. The citta which experiences nibbāna is a "supramundane" citta[16], it is of a plane of citta which is higher than the plane of cittas which experience sense objects or the plane of cittas with absorption. All eight Path factors accompany the supramundane citta at the moment of enlightenment. Defilements are subsequently eradicated at four stages of enlightenment. The supramundane cittas which experience nibbāna arise and then fall away immediately. When the fourth and final stage of enlightenment has not been attained, defilements arise again. However, for the person who has attained enlightenment there are no more conditions to commit akusala kamma to the degree that it can produce rebirth in an unhappy plane of existence.

When one reads the words "enlightenment" and "supramundane", one may imagine that enlightenment is something mysterious, that it cannot occur in daily life. However, it is the function of right understanding to penetrate the true nature of realities in daily life, and when it has been developed to the degree that enlightenment can be attained, the supramundane citta which experiences nibbāna can arise in daily life. Enlightenment can be attained even shortly after akusala citta has arisen, if right understanding has penetrated its true nature. We read in the *Psalms of the Sisters* (Therīgāthā, Canto I, 1) that a woman attained enlightenment in the kitchen. When she noticed that the curry was burnt in the oven she

---
[16] In Pāli: lokuttara citta.

realized the characteristic of impermanence inherent in conditioned realities and then attained enlightenment. Events in daily life can remind us of the true nature of realities. If understanding could not develop in daily life it would not be true understanding. We read that people in the Buddha's time could attain enlightenment even while they were hearing the Buddha preach or just after his sermon. One may wonder how they could attain enlightenment so quickly. They had accumulated the right conditions for enlightenment during innumerable lives and when time was ripe the supramundane cittas could arise.

The development of understanding from the beginning phase to full understanding is an infinitely long process. That is the reason why many different conditioning factors are needed to reach the goal. The study of the teachings, pondering over them, understanding of the way of development of the eightfold Path are conditions for mindfulness and direct understanding of realities. However, apart from these conditions there are others which are essential. Ignorance, clinging and the other defilements are deeply rooted and hard to eradicate. Therefore, in order to reach the goal, the eradication of defilements, all kinds of kusala have to be accumulated together with the development of right understanding. The Buddha developed during innumerable lives, even when he was an animal, all kinds of excellent qualities, the "Perfections". These were the necessary conditions for the attainment of Buddhahood. Also his disciples had developed the Perfections life after life before they could attain enlightenment. Since the accumulation of the Perfections is essential in order to be able to develop the eightfold Path I would like to explain what these Perfections are.

Chapter 8 • The eightfold Path

The ten Perfections are the following:

liberality
good moral conduct
renunciation
wisdom
energy
patience
truthfulness
determination
loving-kindness
equanimity

The Buddha, when he was still a Bodhisatta, developed all these Perfections to the highest degree. For those who see as their goal the eradication of defilements, all these Perfections are necessary conditions for the attainment of this goal, none of them should be neglected.

First of all I wish to give an illustration of the development of the Perfections by the Bodhisatta during the life when he was the ascetic Akitti. We read in the *Basket of Conduct* (Cariyā-piṭaka, I, Conduct of Akitti) that the Buddha spoke about the Perfection of liberality he accumulated in that life. Sakka, King of the Devas (divine beings) of the "Threefold Heaven" came to him in the disguise of a brahman, asking for almsfood. Akitti had for his meal only leaves without oil or salt, but he gave them away wholeheartedly and went without food. We read:

And a second and third time he came up to me. Unmoved, without clinging, I gave as before.
By reason of this there was no discolouration of my physical frame. With zest and happiness, with delight I spent that day.
If for only a month or for two months I were to find a worthy

> *recipient, unmoved, unflinching, I would give the supreme gift.*
> *While I was giving him the gift I did not aspire for fame or gain.*
> *Aspiring for omniscience I did those deeds (of merit).*

Akitti performed this generous deed in order to accumulate conditions for the attainment of Buddhahood in the future. The commentary to this text, the *Paramatthadīpanī*, states that Akitti accumulated all ten Perfections while he was giving his gift.

The Perfection of liberality is developed in order to have less clinging to possessions. We cling to material things because we want the "self" to be happy. If we do not learn to give away material things, how could we ever get rid of clinging to the concept of self? Akitti also accumulated good moral conduct, wholesomeness by action and speech. He was helping the brahman in giving him food. He accumulated renunciation. Renunciation is not merely renunciation of the household life. All kinds of wholesomeness are forms of renunciation, of detachment. One renounces clinging to oneself, to one's own comfort. Akitti renounced his own comfort when he went without food for three days. Akitti accumulated the Perfection of wisdom. The Perfection of wisdom is not only right understanding of the eightfold Path, it comprises all levels of wisdom. The Bodhisatta, even when he was an animal, accumulated the Perfection of wisdom. He knew akusala as akusala, kusala as kusala, he knew the right conditions for the attainment of Buddhahood. When he gave food to the brahman, there was energy or courage, which is indispensable for each kind of kusala. Energy strengthens the kusala citta so that good deeds can be performed. He had patience, he was glad to endure hunger for three days, and had there be an opportunity for a longer period of time to give away his food, he would have fasted longer, even for one or two months. He also accumulated the Perfection of truthfulness. Truthfulness has several aspects. It is not only truthfulness in speech but also sincerity in action and thought. Kusala must be known as kusala and akusala as akusala. One should not delude oneself with regard to one's faults and vices, even when they are more subtle. It should be known that when one is giving a gift with selfish motives, there is no sincere inclination to kusala, that one may take akusala for kusala. Akitti had a sincere inclination to give and did not expect any benefit for himself. The Perfection of truthfulness is indispensable for the development of right understanding. One has to be sincere with regard to what one has understood and what one has not understood yet, otherwise there cannot be any progress. The Bodhisatta accumulated determination, he had an unshakable determination to persevere with the development of understanding and the other Perfections until he would reach the goal. He had loving-kindness, he thought of the brahman's welfare, not of himself. There was equanimity, he had no aversion even though he went without food for three days. He had equanimity towards the vicissitudes of life. Right understanding of kamma and the result of kamma conditions equanimity.

This text illustrates that the Perfections can be accumulated when a good deed is being performed. As we have seen, there are ten kinds of good qualities which have been classified as the Perfections. Good qualities are not always Perfections. They are Perfections only when the aim of the performing of kusala is the diminishing of defilements and eventually their eradication at enlightenment. The accumulation of the ten Perfections together with the development of right understanding of realities is the application of the Buddha's teachings in daily life. There may not be mindfulness of ultimate realities very often, but there are many opportunities to accumulate other kinds of kusala, the Perfections. It is encouraging to know that all kinds and levels of kusala can be Perfections, helpful conditions to reach the goal. Even when we help other people in giving them good advice or in consoling them when they are in distress can be an opportunity for the accumulation of the Perfections, conditions to diminish selfishness and other defilements.

The Development of the eightfold Path which leads to enlightenment seems to be far-fetched for an ordinary person. It is such a long way before the goal can be reached. There will be more confidence in the Buddha's teachings when one sees that what he taught can be verified and applied in one's own life. The development of understanding can only be very gradual, just as learning a new skill such as a foreign language has to be very gradual. The Perfection of patience is indispensable for the development of right understanding of realities. Learning about the Path-factors which each perform their own function helps us to see that no self, no person develops right understanding. We do not have to adopt a particular life-style for the development of understanding. Understanding can develop when it is assisted by the other Path-factors and supported by other conditions, including the Perfections. There should be no discouragement about the long way which lies ahead. There can at least be a beginning of understanding of the reality appearing at the present moment through one of the six doors.

The Buddha taught the conditions for the development of what is good and wholesome and the conditions for the eradication of defilements. In developing the Buddha's Path one will come to know one's ignorance of realities, one's selfishness and other defilements. The change from selfishness to detachment, from ignorance to understanding is immense. How could such changes take place within a short time? It is a long process. Also the Buddha and his disciples had to walk a long way in order to gain full understanding of the four noble Truths and freedom from the cycle of birth and death. We read in the *Kindred Sayings* (V, Kindred Sayings about the Truths, chapter III, §1, Knowledge) that the Buddha said to the monks:

> *Monks, it is through not understanding, not penetrating four noble truths that we have run on, wandered on, this long, long road, both you and I. What are the four?*
>
> *Through not understanding, not penetrating the noble truth of dukkha, of the arising of dukkha, of the ceasing of dukkha, of the way leading to the ceasing of dukkha, we have run on, wandered on, this long road, both you and I.*
>
> *But now, monks, the noble truth of dukkha is understood, penetrated, likewise the noble truth of the arising, of the ceasing of dukkha, of the way leading to the ceasing of dukkha is understood, is penetrated. Uprooted is the craving to exist, destroyed is the channel to becoming, there is no more coming to be…*

Selected texts

from the Pāli Canon

'Straight' is the name that Road is called, and 'Free
From Fear' the Quarter whither thou art bound.
Thy Chariot is the 'Silent Runner' named,
With Wheels of Righteous Effort fitted well.
Conscience the Leaning-board; the Drapery
Is Heedfulness; the Driver is the Norm,
I say, and Right Views, they that run before.
And be it woman, be it man for whom
Such chariot doth wait, by that same car
Into Nibbāna's presence shall they come.

Kindred Sayings 1, v, § 6

...In safety and in bliss
May creatures all be of a blissful heart.
Whatever breathing beings there may be,
No matter whether they are frail or firm,
With non excepted, be they long or big
Or middle-sized, or be they short or small
Or thick, as well as those seen or unseen,
Or whether they are dwelling far or near,
Existing or yet seeking to exist,
May creatures all be of a blissful heart.
Let no one work another one's undoing
Or even slight him at all anywhere;
And never let them wish each other ill
Through provocation or resentful thought.
And just as might a mother with her life
Protect the son that was her only child,
So let him then for every living thing
Maintain unbounded consciousness in being,
And let him too with love for all the world
Maintain unbounded consciousness in being
Above, below, and all around in between,
Untroubled, with no enemy or foe...

Karaniya Mettā-sutta
(Sutta Nipāta, vs. 143-152)

Thus have I heard: On a certain occasion the Exalted One was staying near Sāvatthī, at Jeta Grove in Anāthapiṇḍika's Park. Now at that time the only son, dear and delightful, of a certain lay-follower had died. And a great number of lay-followers, with clothes and hair still wet (from washing), came to visit the Exalted One, and on coming to him saluted him and sat down at one side. As they sat thus the Exalted One said to those lay-followers: 'How is it upāsakas, that ye come here at an unseasonable hour.'

Thereupon the Exalted One, seeing the meaning of it, at that time gave utterance to this verse of uplift:

In bondage to the dear and sweet, many a deva,
  many a man,
Worn with woe, submit themselves to the Lord of
  Death's command.
But they who, earnest night and day, cast aside the
  lovely form,
They dig up the root of woe, the bait of Death so hard
  to pass.

Udāna II, vii

...at Sāvatthī, Sister Vajirā, rising early...plunged into the depths of Dark Wood, and seated herself at the foot of a certain tree for noonday rest. Then Māra the evil one, desirous to arouse fear, wavering, and dread in her, desirous of making her desist from being alone, went up to her, and addressed her in verse:-

By whom was wrought this 'being'? Where is he
Who makes him? Whence doth a being rise?
Where doth the being cease and pass away?

Then Sister Vajirā thought: 'Who now is this, human or non-human, that speaketh verse? Sure 't is Māra the evil one speaketh verse, desirous of arousing in me fear, wavering, and dread, desirous of making me desist from being alone.' And the Sister, knowing it was Māra, replied with verses:-

'Being'! Why dost thou harp upon that word?
'Mong false opinions, Māra, hast thou strayed.
Mere bundle of conditioned factors, this!
No 'being' can be here discerned to be.
For just as, when the parts are rightly set,
The word 'chariot' ariseth [in our minds],
So doth our usage covenant to say:
'A being' when the aggregates are there.

Nay, it is simply Ill that rises, Ill
That doth persist, and Ill that wanes away.
Nought beside Ill it is that comes to pass,
Nought else but Ill it is doth cease to be.

Then Māra the evil one thought: 'Sister Vajirā knows me,' and sad and sorrowful he vanished there and then.

Kindred Sayings 1, v, § 10

No doing of any kind of evil,
Perfecting profitable skill,
And purifying one's own heart:
This is the Buddha's dispensation.
                                        Dhammapada 183

Sorrow disguised as joy, the hateful as the loved,
Pain in the form of bliss the heedless overwhelms.
                                        Udāna II, viii

'Wisdom is best,' the good confess,
Like the moon in starry skies;
Virtue, fortune, righteousness,
Are the handmaids of the wise.
                                        Jātaka 402

Not the unworthy actions of others,
Not their deeds of commission or omission,
But one's own deeds of commission and omission,
Should one regard.
                                        Dhammapada verse 50

Let a man overcome anger by non-anger,
let him overcome evil by good,
let him overcome the miser by liberality,
let him overcome the liar by truth.
                                        Dhammapada 223

Reborn in this Buddha-age through our Bodhisat, as the son of Princess Yasodharā, he was reared with a great retinue of nobles. The circumstances of his entering the Order are recorded in the Khandhaka. And he, his knowledge ripened by gracious words in many Sutta passages, conjured up insight, and so won arahantship. Thereupon, reflecting on his victory, he confessed aññā:

Twice blest of fortune am I whom my friends
Call 'Lucky Rahūla,' for I am both
Child of the Buddha and a Seer of truths;
Yea, and intoxicants are purged from me;
Yea, and there's no more coming back to be.
Ar'hant am I, worthy of men's offerings;
'Thrice skilled' my ken is of ambrosial things.

Blinded are beings by their sense-desires,
Spread o'er them like a net; covered are they
By cloak of craving; by their heedless ways
Caught as a fish in mouth of funnel-net,
But I, that call of sense abandoning,
Have cut and snapt the bonds of devil's lure.
Craving with craving's root abolishing;
Cool am I now; extinct is fever's fire.

Rāhula § 294-298
Psalms of the Brethren,

Passing by

...so standing the deva spoke this verse before the Exalted One:

The hours pass by. Nights drive us ever on.
Stages of life in turn abondon us:
Whoso doth contemplate this fear of death,
Let him so act that merit brings him bliss.

[the Exalted One:]

The hours pass by. Nights drive us ever on.
Stages of life in turn abondon us:
Whoso doth contemplate this fear of death,
Let him reject the bait of all the worlds,
Let him aspire after the final peace.

Kindred Sayings I, text i, 2

The Exalted One said...

'Monks, there is a darkness of interstellar space, impenetrable gloom, such a murk of darkness as cannot enjoy the splendour of this moon and sun, though they be of such mighty magic power and majesty.'

At these words a certain monk said to the Exalted One:

'Lord, that must be a mighty darkness, a mighty darkness indeed! Pray, Lord, is there any other darkness greater and more fearsome than that?'

'There is indeed, monk, another darkness, greater and more fearsome. And what is that other darkness?

Monk, whatsoever recluses or brahamins understand not, as it really is, the meaning of: This is Ill, this is the arising of Ill, this is the ceasing of Ill, this is the practice that leads to the ceasing of Ill, such take delight in the activities which conduce to rebirth. Thus taking delight they compose a compound of activities which conduce to rebirth. Thus composing a compound of activities they fall down into the darkness of rebirth, into the darkness of old age and death, of sorrow, grief, woe, lamentation and despair. They are not released from birth and death...and despair. They are not released from Ill I declare.

But, monk, those recluses or brahmins who do understand, as it really is, the meaning of: This is Ill...such take not delight in the activities which conduce to rebirth. Thus not taking delight they compose not a compound of such activities. Thus not compounding...they fall not down into the darkness of rebirth...old age...sorrow...and despair. They are released therefrom. They are released from ill, I declare

Wherefore, monk, an effort must be made to realize:– This is Ill...'

Kindred Sayings, chapter V, part 6

Glossary

akusala unwholesome, unskilful
anattā not self
anumodana thanksgiving
arahat noble person who has attained the fourth and last stage of enlightenment
Buddha a person who becomes fully enlightened without the aid of a teacher
cetasika mental factor arising with consciousness
citta consciousness, the reality which knows or cognizes an object
dhamma the teachings, the law, reality, truth
dukkha suffering, unsatisfactoriness of conditioned realities
jhāna absorption which can be attained through the development of calm
kamma intention or volition; deed motivated by volition
kasina disk, used as an object for the development of calm
Khandha group of existance
kusala wholesome, skilful
lokuttara citta supramundane citta which experiences nibbāna
nāma mental phenomena
nibbāna unconditioned reality, the reality which does not arise and fall away. The destruction of lust, hatred and delusion. The deathless. The end of suffering.
rūpa physical phenomena
samatha the development of calm
satipaṭṭhāna direct understanding of realities
sīla morality, virtue
Thagātha a fully enlightened person
Tipiṭaka the teachings of the Buddha
vipassanā the development of insight

Index

abhidhamma,
  origin of, 6, 30
absorption, 105, 111
accumulated tendencies, 55
affection, 58
akusala kamma, 69
akusala,
  definition of, 16
  citta, 54
anattā, 36, 129
animals,
  eating, 88
anumodana, 85
arahat, 124
attachment, 56, 58
aversion, 59
awareness, 114

B

behaviour, 64
birth, 77
Bodhi-tree, 12, 13, 16
Bodhisatta, 11
Buddha,
  death of, 12
  birth, 10
  enlightenment, 12
  wife, 10
  teachings, 12
  as God, 10
Buddhaghosa, 38
Buddhahood,
  conditions for, 136
cetasika, 124
charioteer, 11
citta, 129
  definition, 51
  unskilled, 56
  variety of, 56
clinging,
  degrees of, 69
conceit, 86

concentration, 106, 107
  path factor, 129
concept, 45, 113
conception, 77
craving, 17
criminal, 75

D

death,
  as meditation subject, 110
deeds, 67
Deerpark, 27
defilements, 119
Dependent Origination, 80
dhamma, 13, 14, 33
dispersion, 81
dukkha,
  definition of, 27
  sutta on, 131
effort,
  path factor, 128
eight Path factors, 125
eight worldly conditions, 70
eightfold Path, 19, 123
endurance, 60
energy,
  as path factor, 128
  as perfection, 137
enlightenment, 79, 81, 128
  stages of, 124
equanimity, 70, 139
  as perfection 137
evil, 83
extinction (nibbāna), 18
famine, 73
Five groups, 28
five khandhas of clinging, 39
five precepts, 89
food, 98
forbearance, 60
Four Noble Truths, 16, 27
free will, 43

friends, 61
friendship, 109

G

generosity, 56, 68, 84, 85
  as perfection, 137
God, 17, 71
Gotama (Buddha), 10
heaven, 74, 100
hell, 74, 100
Hīnayāna, 12
ignorance, 60
  as factor in Dependent Origination, 80
immorality, 58
insight meditation, 104
insight,
  stages of, 134
Isipatana, 27
Jātakas, 92
jhāna, 105

K

kamma, 83
  definition of, 67
  as abstention, 127
karma,
  definition of, 67
kasinas, 106
Kassapa, Mahā, 95
Khandhas, 28, 32, 79
  of clinging, 39
  not self in, 49
killing, 68, 88
Kisā-gotamī, 23
kusala kamma, 68
kusala,
  definition of, 16
  citta, 54

Kusinārā, 12
laymen,
  precepts of, 89
liberality,
  as perfection, 137
livelihood,
  wrong, 90
  monks, 96
  path factor, 127
lokuttara, 135
lotus, 14
loving-kindness, 60
  development of, 109, 110
Lumbini, 10
lying, 88

M

Mahā Kassapa, 6
Mārā, 42
Māyā (Queen), 10
Mahāyāna, 12
meditation, 103
  subjects of, 106
memory, 134
mental development, 84, 103
mental factors, 56
mental phenomena, 112, 117
middle path, 123
mind, 51
mindfulness, 114, 115
  of breathing, 107
  condition for, 118
  four applications of, 132
  objects of, 133
monkhood, 94
monks,
  robes, 95
  almsfood, 95
moral conduct,
  as path factors, 127
  as perfection, 137

morality,
   development, 129
nāma, 112
nibbāna 124, 135
   definition of, 17
nirvāṇa, 17
Noble Truths 16, 27
non self, 19, 35
nun, 89

P

Pāli Text Society, 7
Pāli, 6
parents,
   as condition for birth, 73
Path of Purification, 7
patience, 128
   for understanding, 140
peace, 73
Perfections, 136, 137
physical phenomena, 112, 117
plane of existence, 74
possessions, 138
prayer, 91
precepts, 89
principles, 101

R

rebirth, 77
refuge,
   teaching as, 10
reincarnation, 79
relaxation, 104
remebrance, 134
roots,
   as support of citta, 57, 62
rude speech, 88
rules,
   of monkhood, 94
rūpa, 112

S

Sahampati (Brahmā), 13
samatha, 104
sati, 114
satipaṭṭhāna, 132
self, 5, 53
senses,
   guarding of, 99
sexual misconduct, 88
Siddhatta, 10
Sigālovāda sutta, 93
Sīha, General, 88
sīla,
   eightfold path, 127
Silent Buddha, 108
sin, 58
sincerity,
   as perfection, 139
slandering, 88
soul, 51
speech,
   as path factor, 127
spirit, 51
stealing, 88
subconsciousness, 55
Suddhodana (king), 10
suffering,
   cause of, 9
Sujātā, 12
supramundane citta, 135
supreme being, see God
Suttanta,
   origin of, 6, 30
talk,
   topics of, 98
Tathāgata, 37
television,
   watching, 133
Theravāda Buddhism, 12
   origin of, 6
thinking, 64, 126, 127
   function of, 127

tranquil meditation, 104
   concentration in, 129
truth,
   conventional and ultimate, 64
   as perfection, 139
ultimate truth, 37-8
understanding, 21
unwholesomeness, 14
Varanasī, 27
vegetarian, 88
Vinaya,
   origin of, 6, 30
   rules for the monks, 94, 95

vipassanā, 104
Vipassi (Buddha), 11
Visuddhimagga, 38

W

war, 73
wisdom, 61
   as perfection, 138
womb, 74
Yasodhāra (Princess), 10

Other Publications

Abhidhamma in Daily Life
By Nina van Gorkom

This unique book takes the reader straight to the higher doctrine of Theravāda Buddhism - the Abhidhamma. It cuts through the complexities of the original texts enabling the reader to obtain a clearer grasp of the theory and practice of the teachings. Many Pāli terms are used in order to bring about a precise understanding of the different realities of our daily life. Suitable for the serious beginner to Buddhism or for advanced students.

1992, 284pp, paperback,
130mm x 190mm,
ISBN 1 897633 01 7,
price £6.95.

Buddhism in Daily Life
By Nina van Gorkom

A general introduction to the main ideas of Theravāda Buddhism. With its many quotes from the Pāli texts, it shows the practical application of the teachings to daily life. The Eightfold Path, the Four Noble Truths, the development of calm and the development of insight are all discussed. Suitable for beginners and experts alike.

1992, 175pp, paperback,
130mm x 190mm,
ISBN 1 897633 02 5,
price £5.95

The World in the Buddhist Sense
By Nina van Gorkom

Explains the world in the Buddhist sense: the realities in and around ourselves. Analyses the difference between the development of calm and the development of insight. Discusses the meditation practice of "mindfulness of breathing". Illustrates with many quotes from the Pāli Tipitaka. Suitable for those who have a background of Buddhism but who seek a deeper understanding.

October 1993, 123 pp,
paperback, 210mm x 140mm.
ISBN 1 897633 11 4,
price £7.95.